neuroscience
and the
FRUIT
of the SPIRIT

BRYAN SPOON, MDIV, BCC

Neuroscience and the FRUIT of the SPIRIT

Copyright © 2020 Bryan Spoon

Cover design by Talva Rogers
Illustrations by Bryan Spoon

https://nrsvbibles.org/index.php/licensing/

* [Scripture quotations are from] New Revised Standard Version Bible, copyright © 1989 National Council of the Churches of Christ in the United States of America. Used by permission. All rights reserved worldwide.

All rights reserved. No part of this book may be reproduced or transmitted in any form or by any means without written permission from the author.

T.A.L.K. Publishing
5215 North Ironwood Road, Suite 200
Glendale, WI 53217
talkconsulting.net

T.A.L.K.
Publishing
TELL.ACCEPT.LEARN.KNOW.
talkconsulting.net

Title: Neuroscience and the Fruit of the Spirit
ISBN: 978-1-952327-13-1

Dedication

I dedicate this book to the many children I minister with as a pediatric chaplain. Despite facing cancer, illness, or disease, these children choose life. They have taught me that each day is a blessing, and they remind me to be playful. I now realize that "simple things" like walking and breathing without pain are miraculous gifts beyond measure. After journeying with so many children who have faced death, I recognize with the most profound urgency that every moment with the people we love is a treasure. Let us choose life and share love abundantly!

Table of Contents

Chapter 1 - You Will Know Them by Their Fruits 11
Chapter 2 - Your Body Is a Temple of the Holy Spirit 17
Chapter 3 - Love vs. Indifference 29
Chapter 4 - Joy vs. Addiction 53
Chapter 5 - Peace vs. Anxiety 69
Chapter 6 - Patience vs. Desperation 83
Chapter 7 - Kindness vs. Hatred 97
Chapter 8 - Goodness vs. Ignorance 109
Chapter 9 - Faith vs. Falsehood 123
Chapter 10 - Gentleness vs. Prejudice 147
Chapter 11 - Self-Control vs. Volatility 157
Chapter 12 - Your Story Is Part of God's Story 171
Chapter 13 - Group Discussion 173
Bibliography of Recommended Reading 177
Glossary 181
Index 191
Notes 193

"This is a really cool book. Virtue meets theology meets neuroscience meets personal growth. As one makes the journey through the book, one learns how fundamental dispositions that lead to a life living the fruit of the Spirit are made possible by this remarkable brain of ours. With exercises at the end of each chapter, this is a book that can be truly transformative. You will not simply know more about yourself, you will be more fully the self that God intended."

The Very Rev. Ian S. Markham, PhD
Dean and President of Virginia Theological Seminary and Professor of Theology and Ethics

"I recommend this fascinating book to all who agree with St. Ignatius—'Our one desire and our one choice should be this: we want and we choose whatever will allow God's life to be deepened in us.' Bryan Spoon has crafted a beautiful integration of neuroscience, the study of emotions, and Christian Scripture and teaching. I will surely use these ideas not only for my own growth but also to enrich adult formation classes."

The Rev. Janice Hicks, BCC
Eldercare Chaplain and coauthor of *Redeeming Dementia: Spirituality, Theology, and Science*

"A creative intersection of Christian thought and neuroscience that offers powerful and pragmatic tools to help you nurture the true self that you deserve."

Jeffrey M Schwartz, MD
Research Psychiatrist and coauthor of *You Are Not Your Brain* and *The Wise Advocate*

"*Neuroscience and the Fruit of Spirit* is a sure guide for understanding the physiological basis for spirituality and ethical behavior. Drawing from his own experience as an Episcopal priest and hospital chaplain, Bryan Spoon offers a dialogue between modern neuroscience and the Bible to reveal the physiological changes that occur when life is centered on love, joy, peace and other fruit of the Spirit (Galatians 5:22–23). He expertly shows how our spiritual practices can literally reshape the brain and lead us to health and wholeness. I strongly recommend this work for both individual and group study."

Wilburn T. Stancil, PhD
Professor Emeritus of Theology at Rockhurst University, Kansas City, Missouri

Chapter 1 - You Will Know Them by Their Fruits

chapter one
You Will Know Them by Their Fruits

Modern neuroscience is shedding incredible light into how our bodies and brains work. It shows how we are transformed by God's love when the fruit of the Spirit courses through us. These are discoveries that we can celebrate for ourselves. They are also discoveries that we can share with others to show them the riches of our faith. What greater treasures are there than love, joy, and peace?

Discoveries in neuroscience are also showing us the physiological systems of how we believe. Belief is mysterious, awesome, and powerful, but many have turned from religion because they do not see people of faith following the way of love. I can believe in healthy eating, but if my belief does not help transform my life into healthy habits, then I will not know what it is to be healthy. A healthy life in Christ is to live by the fruit of the Spirit.

Timothy Jennings's book *The God-Shaped Heart* details with strong research how levels of alcoholism and pornography use are similar or worse among Christians than the larger population. He also demonstrates how lying, cheating, and sexual misconduct are on the rise. We can do better. Much better. We can let others know who we are by our fruit. We can let others know *whose* we are by our fruit.

Christ is very explicit in telling us, "You will know them by their fruits" (Matthew 7:16). If we profess faith but do not live in and by love, then no one will know that we are Christian. Neither will we know what it is to be Christian if we do not have love in our own hearts. In John 15:16, Christ also said, "You did not choose me but I chose you. And I appointed you to go and bear fruit, fruit that will last." What fruit is he talking about? Scripture outlines the fruit of the Spirit as "love, joy, peace, patience, kindness, generosity, faithfulness, gentleness, and self-control" (Galatians 5:22–23). Our bodies and minds are hardwired for living by all the fruit of the Spirit. If we truly live in and appreciate the reality of our bodies and brains, then we can appreciate how the Holy Spirit works through us.

Chapter 2, "Your Body Is a Temple of the Holy Spirit," dives deeper into the beauty and wonder of our bodies. Because we are created in the image of God, we do not have to go any further than looking into and at ourselves to discover how God is already at work through love, joy, and peace. Seeing the intricacy and design of the laws of the universe has brought us closer to God because we have listened and sought how God is already at work throughout the depths of space. God's laws and reality are also at work in us through our neurophysiology. Once we better understand and appreciate the wealth of our bodies, then we can see how we are created for God's purpose. We are created in God's image (Genesis 1:27). We are literally hardwired for love because God is love. True wealth is living in and by love.

In the remaining chapters, I will outline some key features of what happens to our bodies when we allow ourselves to bear the fruit of the Spirit. When our bodies are flooded by feelings of love, patience, or kindness, there are many very real and powerful processes at work. Our bodies are hardwired to love. Being open to the work of the Holy Spirit is a truly transcendent thing, but the Holy Spirit is often seen as remote or ethereal, which leads some Christians to see the Holy Spirit as inaccessible.

This book is an exploration of the beauty and wonder of the Scripture below:

> If you love me, keep my commands. And I will ask the Father, and he will give you another Advocate to help you and be with you forever—the Spirit of truth. The world cannot accept him, because it neither sees him nor

> knows him. But you know him, for he lives with you and will be in you. I will not leave you as orphans; I will come to you. Before long, the world will not see me anymore, but you will see me. Because I live, you also will live. On that day you will realize that I am in my Father, and you are in me, and I am in you. Whoever has my commands and keeps them is the one who loves me. The one who loves me will be loved by my Father, and I too will love them and show myself to them. Anyone who loves me will obey my teaching. My Father will love them, and we will come to them and make our home with them. Anyone who does not love me will not obey my teaching. These words you hear are not my own; they belong to the Father who sent me. All this I have spoken while still with you. But the Advocate, the Holy Spirit, whom the Father will send in my name, will teach you all things and will remind you of everything I have said to you.
>
> (John 14:15–21, 23–26)

The Holy Spirit, our Advocate, is inside us. The Spirit of truth will remain with us forever. What comfort! Of course, another name for the Holy Spirit is the Comforter. With advances in neuroscience, we're starting to develop the language and vocabulary to understand how the Holy Spirit abides in us and courses through us. Love, joy, peace, patience, and all the fruit of the Spirit produce profound neuroscientific and physiological change in our bodies. Modern neuroscience is helping to give us the language to show the gifts of God working in us. An in-depth examination of the Holy Spirit's work in us will remind us of everything that Christ has taught us. It will remind us of the riches and abundance that are available to us. The word evangelism comes from a root that means good news. When we accept the good news for ourselves, then it will naturally flow out of us and invite others into the same riches that we enjoy.

You will note that as I outline chapter by chapter the neuroscience of each particular fruit of the Spirit, such as love, joy, peace, and patience, I also detail an opposite of that fruit of the Spirit. Examples of the contrast include joy versus addiction or peace versus anxiety. Our bodies abundantly reward us for following God's will through a life in Christ. On the contrary, truly the wages of sin are death through destructive processes at work in our bodies such as addiction, anxiety, and hatred. As Christ said, "Every good tree bears good fruit, but the bad tree bears bad fruit. A good tree cannot bear bad fruit, nor can a bad tree bear good fruit" (Matthew 7:17–18). Examining what something is not is an excellent way to better understand what something is. There is substantial research showing that identifying bad habits at work within us is a powerful tool to overcome those habits.[1]

Although this book outlines some key features of what happens to our bodies when we are transformed by our belief through the work of the fruit of the Spirit, we must remember that these pages and resources are only a very small fraction of what is available to us. The ideas in this book are not meant to be exhaustive or the only way of looking at things. Some might argue for different pairings of opposites such as love versus fear rather than love versus indifference. I recommend taking each example for what it is, a tool to see how we are either letting God work through us or how we are not letting God work through us. Each opposite was chosen to highlight a neurological system that works in opposition to the fruit of the Spirit.

The fruit of the Spirit from Galatians 5:22–23 is not the only way God dwells and works through us. This book could have been written on the cardinal virtues of prudence, temperance, fortitude, or justice. Hospitality, humility, and so many other virtues are also expressions of God's love working through us. For the scope of this book, I am only delving into the fruit of the Spirit expressed in Galatians. I do this largely because the fruit of the Spirit outlined by Paul in Galatians is well known to many Christians. There are many other excellent commentaries on the fruit of the Spirit that take it in slightly different directions. Mine are only some of the ways of looking at it.

Before we begin an examination of the fruit of the Spirit, here are two essential points about neuroscience: neuroplasticity and Hebb's Law. First, neuroscience is finding that our minds are capable of significant change. We now know that our neural networks are more plastic, meaning capable of change. Research is finding that "it takes less than two weeks for a neuron to grow new axons and dendrites."[2] For a long time, it was believed that older people could not rewire their brains through new learning. It was believed that habits were more ingrained. Through the work of the fruit of the Spirit in us, our brains have the capacity to rewire even into our advanced years. Secondly, there is Hebb's Law: Neurons that fire together wire together. When we practice something, our neural circuitry strengthens in helping us to remember and carry it out in the future. The more that our neural circuits fire together in healthy ways, the stronger these pathways become. The more that our will and desires are geared toward love and goodness, the more that our whole person will become an expression of God's goodness.

Despite all our efforts, we cannot solely think that action and perseverance will always lead to the results we want. The apostle Paul, whose life overlapped with Jesus in the early first century and whose story has shaped Christians ever since, shared in Romans 7 his struggle that he often did exactly the opposite of what he wanted to do. Paul realized that God's power is made perfect in weakness. None of us is perfect. All of us are frail. All of us have disabilities. All of us will one day die. To accept this reality does not make us weaker, but stronger. Sometimes we need the help of medication such as antidepressants or antianxiety medication. We could all use more professional counseling whether we think we need it or not. We all need the help of medical professionals. This book is not to take the place of medical professionals or medicine but to supplement the excellent care that is offered by them. As one who works in the medical profession, I can attest to the lifesaving measures that bring people hope.

But this book does have a place. There is sickness in our souls from the sickness in our society. There is a lot of bad fruit out there. It creeps into us, and it stinks! This book will give you a greater vocabulary and resources to fight against the sickness around us. It will also give you a vocabulary to help celebrate the work of the Holy Spirit in you. You will also find an in-depth glossary at the end of this book explaining the spiritual dimensions of the various parts of the brain. The glossary will be an excellent tool to see how you are indeed created in the image of God. If you find yourself feeling overwhelmed or confused by the various parts of the brain, you can also go to my website www.neurotheology.info. It has short videos to help you learn more about the work of the fruit of the Spirit in our bodies. The website also has many other helpful resources for your devotional life, for sermon preparation, and links to other neuroscience tools.

The more you see how God's transforming power is working through each part of your system, the more you will see how your belief transforms you into God's goodness and riches. You will be able to help others find more health and wholeness. I pray that after reading and meditating on some of these truths, you will better know that the kingdom of God is within you (Luke 17:21). The Daily Examen, which is explained in chapter 9 of this book, will also help you to claim these riches for yourself by reviewing how God works through you day by day. I pray this book will better prepare you to share the fruit of the Spirit with others. Let us pray that the Holy Spirit gives us new life and new fruit to share with one another. As you move through this book, consider how the almighty, ever-living, great I AM is at work in you. Let us choose life and choose it abundantly.

chapter two
Your Body Is a Temple of the Holy Spirit

> Do you not know that your body is a temple of the Holy Spirit within you, which you have from God, and that you are not your own? ~ 1 Corinthians 6:19

The works of the Holy Spirit through us by the fruit of love, joy, and peace are invaluable gifts that are to be enjoyed and relished. If we cannot see how they work in our bodies, then we will be lost. The human body is a treasure that is infinitely complex and beautiful. Our physiological makeup is a miracle that is incredibly mind-blowing. Our bodies are the greatest treasure discovered in the universe, yet we still often treat them so terribly as if they were garbage.

Reclaiming the value of our human bodies, our temples, also involves reexamining all that we value. We need to shake things up. To retake the treasure that is our body requires reimagining how we measure value. This involves completely reexamining how we understand wealth. True wealth is living in and by love. As we dive into how the fruit of the Spirit works in and through our bodies, we will become ever more aware of this fact.

There are things people value that don't have worth at all. There are entire industries and empires surrounding habits and addictions that have no real worth. Many industries are negative and destructive, but this does not stop people from valuing them. Media sensationalism that invokes violence and fear is just one of many examples. Many industries build up habits in us that are totally worthless.

When wealth is discussed theologically, there are three different ways that people look at it. One is from the poverty perspective. The poverty perspective would see wealth as something to disdain or mistrust. There is also the other extreme of the prosperity perspective, that anything that we earn is ours by right. The middle ground is stewardship theology.[3]

Stewardship theology reminds us that God gives gifts to each of us, but ultimately those gifts are from God and return to God. No matter what we earn or acquire, it returns to God upon our death. Financial resources, if used for the purpose of stewardship, are a wondrous thing. There is nothing wrong with financial resources in themselves. What is wrong is our cultural understanding of what true wealth is.

Money is morally neutral. It is a tool that makes life easier, but it can also make it very difficult. We might measure what people value based on where they spend their time and money. These are two excellent ways of looking at what people value. A peek at your bank statement or an honest look at your calendar will tell you something about what you value. Looking into the habits and tendencies of our bodies is the clearest way to see what we truly value and hold dear.

Each day the news shows the stock market indexes. People often judge themselves and others by where they live, what money they make, what car they drive, and so many other status symbols. The problem is where many people place their priorities and what they consider treasure. Too many of us have become possessed by our possessions. We need a completely new way of viewing what wealth is. The only way of doing this is to *get our house in order.*

In Hebrew, the word for temple is also the word *house* (Strong's #1004 - בַּיִת). So, let's get our house, our temple, in order! In Greek, the word *economy* is "*oikonomia* meaning 'household management' from *oikonomos* 'manager or steward' and oikos 'house or dwelling.'"[4] At its most basic level, our understanding of economy is first and foremost about how we relate to the temples of our bodies. A temple is sacred. It is set apart and holy. Our greatest resource is our human body. It is the only real resource we will ever know or by which we will ever know anything else. Our bodies are created in the image of God and therefore hardwired for love, for God is love.

Our experience of reality is filtered through electrochemical signals in our bodies. This is true for all of us. It is our prioritization and emotional connection to certain signals versus others that dictate what we value. Is there any other way to experience wealth but through our bodies? Let yourself linger on that question and inwardly digest it. It took me a very long time to realize this, and many of us have trouble appreciating this very important fact. From an electrochemical level, love is the richest and most excellent treasure. It is so tragic that those who don't have it try to convince everyone else of the value of their internal poverty.

Wealth is intimately tied to our emotions because it is our body and mind that interpret any and all things that occur in the outside world. One example of this is how emotion is a vital component of decision-making. It is through connection with our body and our feelings that we make decisions. The deepest motivator and emotion of connection is love, yet many of us are disconnected from our emotional processes. Many of us are extremely far removed from the very temple that God has entrusted to us.

So, what kind of temple or house are we living in?

The human body is infinitely beautiful and wondrously made. It is composed of tens of trillions of cells. Tens of trillions! That number is so enormously large that you probably just read it without truly contemplating how large it is. To put a trillion in perspective, imagine for a moment how long it would take to count to one billion. It would take thirty-one years if you started counting right now. To count to one trillion, it would take one thousand times that long! To make that number even more mind-boggling, you should also remember that each of our cells has within them our DNA, which contains more than three billion base pairs of encoded information.

The human brain, with approximately one hundred billion neurons, has so many connections that they are almost infinite. In

Chapter 2 - Your Body Is a Temple of the Holy Spirit

fact, the human brain is the most complex thing known in the universe. To think of yourself as just a body does not nearly give it justice. You are an ecosystem. You are a vast sprawling universe of infinite complexity and beauty. This is a truth that should leave our jaws dropping to the floor. We should be flabbergasted like someone who just won tens of billions of dollars in the lottery. Each one of us is like a cosmic lottery winner. Even some of the staunchest of atheists believe that last statement. Your consciousness is like being the CEO of a galaxy composed of hundreds of billions of stars. In the exquisitely vast expanse of space, we are the most complex and rarest thing yet to be discovered. Wow!

Many people value rare items like gems. Gems like diamonds and emeralds can be worth thousands of dollars. Our bodies are the rarest and most complex things known in the universe, far more precious than any gemstone, but we often treat them like garbage! If you owned several diamonds or emeralds, would you treat them like garbage? If you had a winning lottery ticket worth billions of dollars, would you throw it in the trash?

Each one of us is fearfully and wonderfully made. The next time you are together with a big group, I challenge you to take time to notice how unique each person is. Not one is the same as another. Not even an identical twin will be the same as another. I believe this is one of the most significant pieces of evidence for the existence of God. That we are not all the same is extremely profound. God loves each one of us so much that we are infinitely unique. There is even a part of the brain, the fusiform face area, that helps us distinguish the uniqueness of others, especially by their faces. It is located on the underside of the temporal lobe. Each one of us is wonderfully made, and God has given us the gift to help recognize it.

Have you been to the Statue of Liberty? I was there years ago. I took the tour where you can go up to the pedestal. From the pedestal, you can walk these little steps until you get to the very top of the statue. It's a little bit strange to be inside of her head. From the inside vantage of the stairs, you can see the various metal sheets that make up the landmark. When you finally get to the top of the statue, you're in her crown. There is an incredible view of New York

Neuroscience and the FRUIT of the SPIRIT

from that vantage point. It's a breathtaking sight, but it's also kind of strange. Looking out of her crown so high up, you can also see her arm extending out. It's almost as if you're seeing out of her eyes. You can have the feeling that you are somehow just as large as she is. Each of us is like a Statue of Liberty. Yes, this might sound like a strange idea, but is it much different from 1 Corinthians 6:19, which asks, "Do you not know that your body is a temple of the Holy Spirit?" Scripture reminds us that we are a temple of the Holy Spirit. Honestly, I forget sometimes. Really, I often forget this.

To consider our bodies as something as grand and magnificent as the Statue of Liberty might make us feel uneasy. It might make us feel prideful or fearful of putting too much stock in ourselves. But is it prideful to see ourselves as beautiful as the Statue of Liberty? By some calculations, there are more atoms in the human body than there are known stars in the universe. Maybe that's still unconvincing. Perhaps it sounds a bit crazy to think of yourself to be as grand as the Statue of Liberty. I might ask, is it not crazier to deny how incredibly and infinitely complex you are considering how much we know about the universe?

I'd like to invite you to take a moment to marvel at the majesty of our universe. Picture the sun in your mind. Now picture the Earth. They both might seem very large, but the sun is so much bigger than the Earth that it is staggering. In fact, over one million Earths could fit inside of the sun.[5] One million!

Here is another truly awesome illustration of the immensity of our universe. According to NASA, there are over two trillion galaxies within our universe.[6] In our galaxy, the Milky Way, there are approximately 100 to 400 billion stars.[7] And yet, human beings are the most complex and preciously rare things we have discovered in the entire universe!

Having looked at it from the large, let's look at how immeasurably infinite each one of us is from a smaller scale. Have you heard of the Butterfly Effect? In 1961, scientist Edward Lorenz was computing weather models when he found that the slightest difference in an initial query running simulations ultimately produced extremely different weather patterns. The concept later became known as the Butterfly Effect. There have been many different iterations of it, but the principle is that something as small as a butterfly that beats its wings in Brazil can have the effect of ultimately producing a hurricane in Texas. If the butterfly is beating its wings elsewhere at another moment, the effect over time will indeed produce drastically different weather patterns even halfway across the world. Each one of us, no matter how small we seem in our own minds, is infinitely powerful. The simple act of helping a person feel affirmed and loved might seem like something small, but each moment has an infinite impact. Truly.

Even with all the evidence that we are wondrously made, rather than marveling at how incredibly intricately we are designed or how immeasurably powerful we are, we often treat our bodies and minds like trash. We often see ourselves as defective or, at best, ordinary, when in fact, we are *the most* extraordinary thing humanity has discovered in the entire universe.

Many things that people value are based on addiction: power, sensationalism, fame, traumatic news, materialistic wealth, social status, overindulging, etc. We can focus on that which builds up the economy of our temples. To build up God's kingdom is to build up our own personal temple as well as to build up goodness on earth. We are reminded in 1 Corinthians 8:1, "Knowledge puffs up, but love builds up." *To build up* (Strong's #3618 - οἰκοδομέω) also means to found, establish, or grow in wisdom. Remember that in Greek, the word *economy* means household management. Let us manage the temples of our bodies by being established in truth and goodness.

Christ also uses the example of building up a house in his parable of the wise and foolish builders:

> Therefore, everyone who hears these words of mine and puts them into practice is like a wise man who built his house on the rock. The rain came down, the streams rose, and the winds blew and beat against that house; yet it did not fall, because it had its foundation on the rock. But everyone who hears these words of mine and does not put them into practice is like a foolish man who built his house on sand. The rain came down, the streams rose, and the winds blew and beat against that house, and it fell with a great crash. (Matthew 7:24–27)

To hear the words of Christ and to put them into practice is to live a life of love, kindness, peace, and joy. This is how we build up our house on the rock. This is true wealth.

The prophet Nehemiah was able to rebuild the walls of Jerusalem in just fifty-two days (Nehemiah 6:15). If each of us took fifty-two days to intentionally refocus and reprioritize our lives, then the temples of our bodies could be raised as the walls of Jerusalem were raised.

If our actions are consistently prideful, arrogant, or sinful, then our lives will lack God's goodness and peace. According to Aristotle, we are largely what we repeatedly do. But who we are is much more than what we do. Our faith in God is about reestablishing *whose* we are, not just our actions. Our faith is about opening ourselves, our temples, up to the work of the Holy Spirit to bear fruit that will last. Each of us has different gifts, and all of us have disabilities. The challenge is not to get stuck on how much we are doing, but to do what we can with what is available to us.

No matter how much we do, grace is at the heart of Christ's teaching. Grace is our foundation and starting point. It is only by God's grace that we can find union with God. Constant striving is a neurosis known as a type A personality. The neurosis of constant doing is also known as joyless striving. Good theology will not propel us to simply be fruit producers as if we're a grocery store or fruit stand. Christ reminds us, "Abide in me as I abide in you. Just as the branch cannot bear fruit by itself unless it abides in the vine, neither can you unless you abide in me. I am the vine, you are the branches" (John 15:4–5).

Constantly judging ourselves and others by how much output we produce is not healthy. As someone who has faced chronic pain for years, which has often been debilitating, I have gone through my own struggles of feeling inadequate. I have had to struggle with knowing that it is not how much I do but the conviction in my heart to do everything that I can. It is also the surrender to God's grace rather than my own merit that is the wellspring of God's gifts. I might not have the strength that I once had. I might not have the mental stamina. I might not have much to give, but if I can give my heart and conviction to God, then it is more than sufficient. I am enough. Each one of us is enough.

Christ drives this point home in this example:

> A poor widow came and put in two small copper coins, which are worth a penny. Then he called his disciples and said to them, "Truly I tell you, this poor widow has put in more than all those who are contributing to the treasury. For all of them have contributed out of their abundance; but she out of her poverty has put in everything she had, all she had to live on." (Mark 12:42–44)

Scripture also reminds us that we will enter the kingdom through the eyes of a child (Matthew 19). Children don't usually have the resources to raise funds or organize a government. What they do have and what they offer is sufficient to know and enter the kingdom of God. That we can do likewise through their example of innocence and joy is sufficient. Having been a pediatric chaplain for the last four years, I have spent much time with children who face the severest developmental delays and challenges. I have spent time with children who are unable to walk, talk, or carry on like a more highly functioning child. What many of these children have is an enormous appreciation for the most basic of life's functions. The joy of smiling, a simple touch, of walking, or simply to breathe provides so much joy and satisfaction to many of these children. They are incredible teachers. If everyone could relish God's gifts of grace as these children do, I believe our world would be a much better place.

Like the immeasurable joy of a child, who we are is not a matter of what we have been or who we think we are. When we accept God as sovereign, we surrender our self to God. To surrender to God is to say, I am Yours. It is choosing to be obedient to God's will.

The idea of surrender might seem terribly scary in a world that values human freedom so highly. The word surrender brings together *sur*, meaning over, and *render*, which means to give, cause, or become. Giving ourselves over to God's grace causes change in us. Through surrender, we become something new. Surrender helps us move into a new reality. When we cook and render the fat, we are clarifying or changing it from what it had been. Surrendering and being obedient to God is the wellspring of our union with God. We cannot have union with God unless we are willing to open ourselves up and let God's goodness fill us.

This book is largely about going deeper into the meaning and power of words. Words are more than concepts. They are doorways of perception. They are anchors of truth. They are the keys to a better future. Truly understanding what a particular word means is very transformative. Let us look at the word grace. Grace is generally defined as unmerited favor. But what is favor? Favor is receiving and relishing what is pleasing, good, wholesome, kind, approved, or supported. What we receive from God is not ours but a gift that we have to enjoy. Surrendering to God is not about slavery. Surrendering to God is about saying yes to friendship with the Lord of life. God gives us life through grace. The word obedience comes from the word obey, meaning to listen.

If we can listen to what is going on inside our bodies, we will see that we are hardwired for love. To follow God's will is to follow a life rooted in love. John 14:15 tells us, "If you love me, you will keep my commandments." We lose who we had been, but we are not giving anything up. We are allowing our whole perspective to shift toward loving the Creator of all, loving others, and loving ourselves. We replace our own character, the I, with the characteristics and gifts of God through love, peace, joy, and wonder. These things are good and pleasing. They are God's favor toward us and also God working in us.

When we surrender to God and say I am Yours, we can see that it is the great I AM working in us. That is who we really are. The Rev. Dr. Steven Rottgers in his book *I am Yours*, elaborates how important this movement is.[8] To say I am Yours to God is about giving up our control. As Scripture tells us, "So if anyone is in Christ, there is a new creation: everything old has passed away; see, everything has become new! All this is from God, who reconciled us to himself through Christ, and has given us the ministry of reconciliation" (2 Corinthians 5:17-18). When we say to God, I am Yours, then all that is old can fall away.

Often an economy is measured by the fruit it produces. It is measured by its treasure. Neuroscience has given us the tools to share the immeasurable wealth of the fruit of the Spirit that courses through our bodies. If each of us has a better vocabulary to know and appreciate the riches that God has hardwired into our very being, then we can communicate and cherish that wealth even more. We can share that wealth with others. Who does not want more love, joy, and peace? What better riches are there?

Christ tells us, "You will know them by their fruits" (Matthew 7:16). With modern neuroscience, we can better name and celebrate the work of the fruit of the Spirit in us. While we're neither meant to quantify love perfectly or to judge ourselves and others by who produces the most love, what we can do is reframe our focus of wealth, value, and treasure. Neuroscience is an outstanding tool to help us do this. In chapter 9 of this book, "Faith vs. Falsehood," you will find the Daily Examen. It is a short reflection to become familiar with how God is working in our lives. It is an excellent tool to help us abide in and relish the riches of the fruit of the Spirit day by day. It also reminds us that our wealth is tied intimately with our bodies. Through practice, we will become better at paying attention to our bodies. We can improve the discernment of our neural processes and acquire the vocabulary to name them. We will also be able to recognize changes over time. Through habitual use of the Daily Examen, we can invite the fruit of the Spirit to work in us and also overcome our habitual bad fruit. When we can feel that our anxiety has gone down and that we are experiencing more love, then we can claim it. We can celebrate it! If we feel and reflect that our anxiety is high, then we can look for tools and resources to reduce and overcome it. We can also observe with less reactivity the painful and damaging processes at work in our bodies so that they do not control us. We can ask ourselves and loved ones to help us find more love, joy, and peace. If we take the time to ask why there is little peace in our lives through a Daily Examen, then we can strive for more peace. We can start seeing the world through the riches of the fruit of the Spirit rather than cultural measures of wealth that do not truly provide us more joy or love. True riches are God's riches of love, joy, and peace.

To consider our bodies as ordinary is one of the largest foundations of poverty in our world. To get mired in addiction or habits that tear us away from the reality that we are the most complex and wondrous thing yet discovered in the universe is extremely tragic. Christ came that we may have life and have it abundantly. If we treasure how God has made us and nurture the systems that are already hardwired into our very being, then we will be tremendously wealthy.

The work of the Holy Spirit in us is a stream of living water. When we let ourselves appreciate and deeply feel love and joy, then we understand how abundantly rich God's treasure is. The electrochemical currents moving through us are the only real wealth that we will ever know or by which we can know anything. Coursing through us is goodness, wonder, and love. Coursing through us is the truth that we are the most complex and wondrous thing yet to be known in the universe. In so many cases, we have been duped into paying attention to electrochemical signals that cause us more suffering or the suffering of others. We can break free and help others to break free, too.

In the following chapters, I will show how each fruit of the Spirit working in our bodies is indeed an incredible treasure. Our bodies abundantly reward us through following God's will through a life in Christ. God's grace and favor are already hardwired into our being. We need not look any further than ourselves to find these treasures. I think this is partly what Jesus meant when he said: "Not everyone who says to me, 'Lord, Lord,' will enter the kingdom of heaven, but only the one who does the will of my Father in heaven" (Matthew 7:21). When our minds and bodies align with love, then they also align with the light. To align with darkness, either in heaven or on earth, will keep us cloaked in darkness. That is why, truly, we will be known and come to know ourselves as children of God through the fruit of the Spirit. When we enter the light, then we produce fruit of and from the Lord of life. And it is rich.

Chapter 2 - Your Body Is a Temple of the Holy Spirit

chapter three
Love vs. Indifference

> The opposite of love is not hate, it's indifference. The opposite of art is not ugliness, it's indifference... And the opposite of life is not death, it's indifference. ~ Elie Wiesel

> Beloved, let us love one another, because love is from God; everyone who loves is born of God and knows God. Whoever does not love does not know God, for God is love. ~ 1 John 4:7–8

Love (Greek – ἀγάπη – *pronounced ah-**gah**-pey*)

The Habit of Love

What is love? Is love sacrifice or affection? Is it both? Is it erotic, or is it a form of friendship? Is it mercy, compassion, courageousness, vulnerability, or empathy? Is it all of these? Is it justice? What is tough love, and how does it differ from unconditional love? Should love be directed to the stranger or to those more familiar? The particular word used for love in Galatians 5:22–23 is ἀγάπη (agape). The definition of ἀγάπη in *Strong's* or *Thayer's Dictionary* is generally "brotherly love, affection, goodwill, love, benevolence."[9] Beyond this simple definition, some define agape more along the lines of self-sacrifice, while others stress affinity or affection. We already see that there is much room for debate, and we're only just scratching the surface! The concept of love is as imprecise as it is central to who we are. The ancient Greeks had several ways of categorizing love: *erao*, "to be in love with, to desire passionately or sexually"; *phileo*, "to have affection for"; *agapao*, "to have regard for, be contented with," and *stergo*, "used especially of the love of parents and children."[10] *Merriam-Webster* defines agape simply as love, eros as self-gratifying or erotic love, and philia as friendship love.[11]

One way of viewing the self-sacrifice of agape is to replace our desire with God's desires for us. In our culture, there is much talk about freedom. But what is freedom? Cicero described it as participation in power. Many of the things that we are invited to participate in that are part of culture might not truly give us more freedom but instead draw us into more servitude. I might be invited to have more power to purchase through a credit card, but ultimately this participation produces huge debt, which will shackle me. Replacing our will with God's will gives us freedom from addictions and things that are not good for us. God's will for us gives us freedom for goodness, righteousness, wonder, and, most especially, love. Freedom involves commitment. The longer and deeper we draw into a real commitment in serving and loving God, the greater freedom for goodness we receive. When we are good, then the goodness courses through us neurologically. It is freedom for receiving God's goodness by feeling and experiencing this very goodness. In the Hebrew Bible, the word חֶסֶד (Strong's #2617), pronounced *hesed* in English, signifies this kind of love. It is love in action. It is mercy. But we can go deeper. Love is tangible. To say I love you without also showing how I love you is not really to love you at all.

Christ says that you will know his disciples by their fruits (Matthew 7:16). We are called to fill ourselves with the fruit of the Spirit, such as love, joy, and peace (Galatians 5:22–23). The fruit of the Spirit is a tangible way that we can express love. In this way, it is an emptying of ourselves of what is not of God, such as sin and bad habits. If we empty ourselves, we can allow God to fill us through the power of the Holy Spirit (Acts 1:8). God can fill us with thanksgiving, grace, and love, which are all things that come from God. We can then become a living sacrifice of praise and thanksgiving, loving others in mutual affection (Romans 12:1–13).

The Neuroscience of Love

To understand what it is to love another, we need to understand what something is for ourselves. This is the most basic element of empathy. Love begins in empathy. Unless we can enter into the emotional reality of others, there is no room for love. Allowing yourself to be affected by another person tears down the wall that has kept you separated. We discover in our connection that the other and ourselves are, in fact, one and the same.

Jesus said that the law and prophets hung on the Great Commandment that we are to love God with all our heart, mind, and soul. We are also to love our neighbor as ourselves (Matthew 22:37–40). From this starting point, we surrender to God. In our surrender, we commit ourselves to love others as we commit to loving ourselves. We are engaged in God's mission of bringing the entirety of reality into the will of God. In the gospels, Jesus is quoting from Deuteronomy 6:5, which says, "You shall love the Lord your God with all your heart, and with all your soul, and with all your might." The word translated as *heart* is from לְבָב (Strong's #3824). This word means both heart and mind, though it is generally only translated as heart. Our mind, body, spirit, and will are one, and are not to be separated. The word translated as *might* is מְאֹד (Strong's #3966). Its meaning is also rich. It means might, but also strength or even our very suchness. Suchness might seem a strange concept, but it signifies our very being. We are to love God, self, and neighbor with our very being. This is far more than mental acceptance. It is being transformed into new life. Entering this place of connection changes us. We are moved from one mindset to another.

This is what Jesus meant when he said, "Blessed are the pure in heart" (Matthew 5:8). When our hearts and minds are geared toward love, then we see and know love. Love becomes our guidepost and lens for the world. For God is love. Another example is from Luke

17:21 when Jesus said that the kingdom of God is within (ἐντός) you. Within us is the hardwiring for love.

Below are five primary ways that God's reign of love is hardwired into our very being. These biological processes are strengthened through love toward God, our neighbors, and ourselves.

Anterior Cingulate Cortex (ACC)

Belief in a cold, harsh, and distant God produces in us fear and aggression. To believe in a cold and critical God activates the limbic system and particularly the amygdala. The amygdala is an almond-shaped structure in the brain that is responsible for the detection and response to threats. If we believe in a cold and distant God, then fear and despair will be our reality.

Acting as a sort of fulcrum between our emotional limbic system and the logical prefrontal cortex is an area of our brain known as the anterior cingulate. It has been called the heart of our brain because when our thoughts, actions, and worldview are fixed on love and loving relationships, this part of the brain is strengthened and activated.[12] Through it, we are wired for love and connection. Its unique cells called von Economo neurons are extensive and guide us to positive emotions. Prolonged anger and anxiety will impair the function of the anterior cingulate.

The ACC also plays a significant part in the process of emotions. It helps you process God as kind and loving. It regulates spiritual anxiety, guilt, anger, and fear. It helps in your understanding of empathy and compassion. Self-discipline and acts of love will strengthen the ACC. Intense and prolonged fear or addictions will weaken it. It plays a large role in listening to the brain's circuitry toward the fear response or choosing the governance of the prefrontal cortex's inhibition of the limbic system. It is a mediator between our feelings and our thoughts. A stronger ACC will help slow down the amygdala's role in the fear response.

Prefrontal Cortex

The front part of the frontal lobe is known as the prefrontal cortex, and it is very important to your integration of self. In *How God Changes Your Brain,* Andrew Newberg and Mark Robert Waldman

Neuroscience and the FRUIT of the SPIRIT

demonstrate through research and imaging how the frontal lobe "creates and integrates all your ideas about God—positive or negative."[13] If the concepts that govern our minds are powerful, then they will help synchronize all of our other bodily systems and integrate our prefrontal cortexes.

Love is the most powerful and positive of all concepts. It is the nature of God. At the heart of love is connection. Our brain circuitry will form connection and deepen if our thoughts are fixed on our union with God.

Three areas of the frontal lobe that are empowered and empower our union with God are the dorsolateral prefrontal cortex, orbitofrontal cortex and the ventromedial prefrontal cortex. The orbitofrontal cortex (OFC) is associated with inhibiting inappropriate social behaviors. It works in conjunction with the anterior cingulate cortex (ACC), especially regarding coordination of emotional reaction. The ventromedial prefrontal cortex (VMPFC) is involved in moral and ethical decision-making as well as making meaning of life. The dorsolateral prefrontal cortex (DLPFC) is the area of the frontal lobe that is responsible for our executive function. There is much research showing that the innermost values that we continually focus on will indeed reframe, strengthen, and restructure our brains.[14]

We are empowered by thoughts and conceptions of God's love for us and our union with God. The prologue of John's gospel reminds us of the union of God and the Word: "In the beginning was the Word, and the Word was with God, and the Word was God" (John 1:1). The Word is with God and is God. This is not a distant or harsh God. This is the God of love revealed to us in Christ. The God of love is also with us. Another name for our Lord is Emmanuel, which means "God is with us." Scripture reminds us of our togetherness with God. Without concepts that ground us in this love, we will be lost from the start. Fear and threat will hijack our amygdala if we are not grounded in the reality of love. Fear will prevent us from utilizing our executive function and our prefrontal cortex.

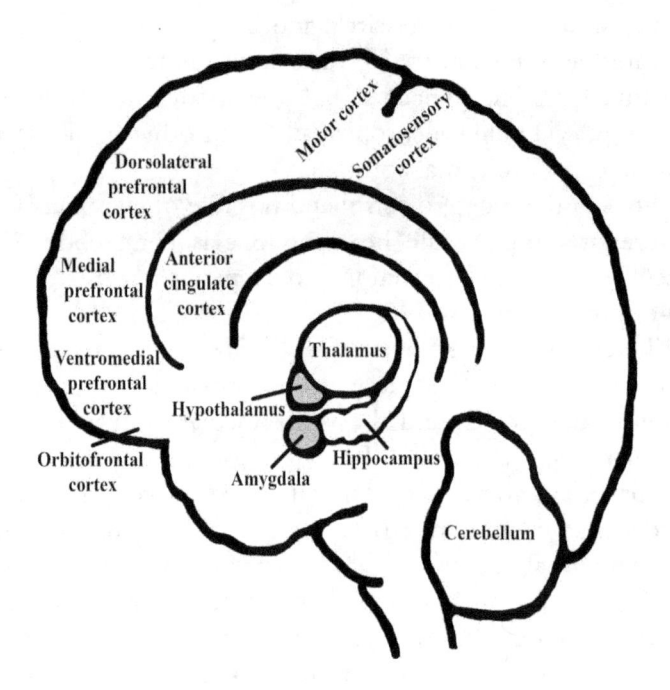

[Brain diagram with labels: Dorsolateral prefrontal cortex, Medial prefrontal cortex, Ventromedial prefrontal cortex, Orbitofrontal cortex, Anterior cingulate cortex, Motor cortex, Somatosensory cortex, Thalamus, Hypothalamus, Amygdala, Hippocampus, Cerebellum]

INSULA AND SOMATOSENSORY CORTEX

The insula helps us interpret our emotions. Imaging has shown that the right frontal insular cortex connects with an ability to empathize with the pain of others. Imaging also shows that it plays a role in the ability to feel one's own bodily organs, such as the heartbeat. It helps us with greater self-awareness through connecting how our emotions are processed in the body. "The insula detects body states that are induced by emotions as part of a process that brings our emotional experiences into our consciousness."[15]

Another area of the brain that helps us connect with feelings all over the body is the somatosensory cortex of the parietal lobe. It contains a sensory map of all the areas of feeling over your body, such as the face, hands, and legs. If we are angry or afraid and we have a strong connection to our body, then we will feel things like our jaw clenched or our palms sweating.

Other bodily states that connect with our emotions might include knots in our stomach, a sense of lightness, goosebumps, flushed cheeks, or feeling heavy and off-center. Certain bodily states connect with certain emotional states. Unless we take the time to understand how our emotions feel in our own bodies, we will never be able to appreciate the emotional experience of another person.

If we are mindfully aware of our body's sensations, then it will strengthen our insula. It will strengthen our empathy.

This concept is so important. At the end of the each section on the fruit of the Spirit, there is a focus question to help you *feel* how the particular fruit of the Spirit or bad fruit is working in your body. With greater knowledge of the bodily sensations working in us, we will have greater awareness of the riches working in us. We will also be able to help other people name and celebrate how the fruit of the Spirit is working in their bodies.

You might wonder why it would be helpful to take time to examine how our negative thoughts and experiences make us feel. There are exercises in this book to help you investigate indifference, anxiety, desperation, and hate. We are often unaware of our negative thoughts and feelings because of past trauma or from habit. Taking the time to slow down and internally observe our destructive patterns helps us label them and overcome them. It can also help us invite others to do the same.

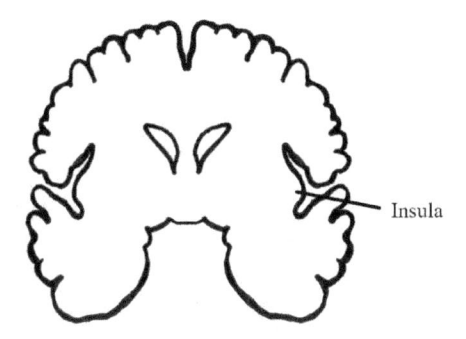

Insula

OXYTOCIN

Oxytocin is a neuropeptide. It helps us feel safe and secure. The release of oxytocin from the hypothalamus helps drop the level of cortisol stress hormones. This also helps blood pressure drop. A soothing and warm touch helps the process unfold. It is not necessary to have touch, however. The connection of your mind and heart to remembering that you are loved and connected has a similar effect. Dan Goleman, in his book *Social Intelligence*, speaks to how we can condition the release of oxytocin by putting ourselves in the proximity of people we feel safe and secure with. There have been studies that show that time with our pets, especially dogs, can help build and strengthen the release of oxytocin. When we activate a memory or image in our mind, we activate the prefrontal cortex. The feeling of being secure and loved within these images and memories will strengthen the circuits to release oxytocin.

Our relationship, bond, affection, and security in God are also rewarded by oxytocin. Our love of God draws us toward altruism, security, bonding, and greater acceptance of out-groups, which are all features of increased levels of oxytocin. Fr. Pedro Arrupe captures the effect well in this poem:

> Nothing is more practical than
> finding God, that is, than
> Falling in Love
> in a quite absolute, final way.
> What you are in love with,
> what seizes your imagination,
> will affect everything.
> It will decide
> what will get you out of bed in the morning,
> what you do with your evenings,
> how you spend your weekends,
> what you read, whom you know,
> what breaks your heart,
> and what amazes you with joy and gratitude.
> Fall in love, stay in love,
> and it will decide everything.[16]

Neuroscience and the FRUIT of the SPIRIT

PARIETAL LOBE

One of the four lobes of the cerebral cortex, the parietal lobe's circuitry with other parts of the brain plays a very significant role in our feeling of union with God. It helps establish our understanding of self with space, time, and objects. The parietal-frontal circuit in particular helps establish a relationship between our conceptions of self and God.[17] It helps establish the feeling of God's presence in time and space as well as our connection to this reality.

The more we pray and meditate on God's presence, the more it becomes real. Intense prayer on the oneness of God and our connection to all things helps decrease activity in the parietal lobe and leads to an increased sense of selflessness. Through prayer and meditation, there is more of an awareness of "we" rather than simply just "I." Rather than being egocentric, our mind can alter our perception of self so that we see ourselves as part of all things. People often, consciously or unconsciously, think about their divisions. Because the parietal lobe is involved in understanding relationships in time and space, concentrating on division in the world will produce more activity in the parietal lobe associated with those divisions. With so many societal distinctions that focus on separation and difference (i.e., conservative/liberal, black/white, communist/capitalist, etcetera), the ability to overcome division is critical to our ability to engage in empathy and love.

Neuroscience helps to show how our connection to God's oneness works in our brains through the parietal-frontal circuit. Our belief and God's grace draw us into this union. It changes our neurophysiological makeup. We can see that when we enter into union with God, we are indeed changed. Christ does not separate his community from himself. It has changed and become part of him. As the apostle Paul said, "It is no longer I who live, but it is Christ who lives in me" (Galatians 2:20).

This same point is beautifully detailed in our previous example from the gospel of John: "Those who love me will obey my teaching. My Father will love them, and we will come to them and make our home with them" (John 14:23). Continued prayer, action, and reflection that strengthens our connection with the oneness of God will continue to strengthen our parietal-frontal circuit so that we may live more deeply in and by this incredible truth. God will make a home in us. Love makes a home in us.

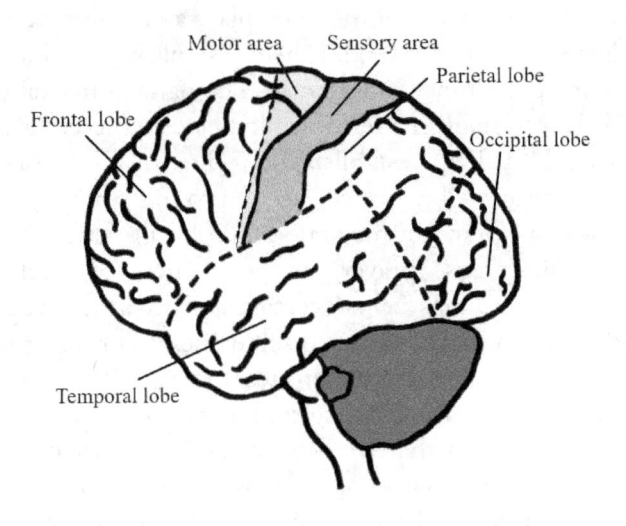

Diagram of brain with labels: Motor area, Sensory area, Parietal lobe, Frontal lobe, Occipital lobe, Temporal lobe

Love: A Theological Perspective

God is love (1 John 4:8). This is one of the simplest yet most profound statements in the entire Bible. Equally exciting is the Scripture that reminds us that we are created in the image of God (Genesis 1:27). Our makeup is geared toward love, for God is love. The ultimate reality and our spiritual home are union with God. Love is our response to the frailties and horror of the world. Love heals divisions. Love draws us to engage and embrace our enemies.

Our freedom, God's gift to us, is given with the risk that we will not love and obey God's will. It is because there is a choice that there is love. If we had to obey God, then there would be no expression of love. There would be no relationship. But if we surrender to God, then we can become fertile ground for God's grace to dwell. We can become filled with the gifts of the Holy Spirit in love, joy, peace, and gentleness. With courage, we can expose ourselves and be vulnerable, opening ourselves up to risk.

If we offer love or joy to the world, it may not be accepted. We may be rejected. We will get wounded. It is not a matter of if we will get wounded but when. If we live by risking our love over and over, we will get wounded. Over and over. But our wounds, like the wounds of Christ after his resurrection, make us wiser and more loving rather than more callous.

Jesus says in Mark 12:31, "You shall love your neighbor as yourself." This commandment can also be found in the Old Testament, Leviticus 19:18, "You shall love your neighbor as yourself." The Hebrew word used is אָהַב, meaning to love God, friend, or family member, or simply as human love.[18] In both these commandments, we are reminded to love our neighbors as ourselves. It is not simply love of neighbor, but ourselves that we are also to love. Perhaps the most beautiful summary of love can be found in 1 Corinthians 13:4–7: "Love is patient; love is kind; love is not envious or boastful or arrogant or rude. It does not insist on its own way; it is not irritable or resentful; it does not rejoice in wrongdoing but rejoices in the truth. It bears all things, believes all things, hopes all things, endures all things." If we are to seriously follow Christ's commandment of loving our neighbors as ourselves, we first need to apply this list to ourselves. Am I rude to myself? Am I patient with myself?

Unless we are willing and open to receive love ourselves, we will not be able to share love with others. We can receive God's love for us by saying yes to God. We can say yes to joy, peace, patience, and kindness. When we start to give ourselves over to God's work, then God will begin working in us. This is real participation in power, God's power working through us. It is the power of love.

A strong indicator of whether we are willing or unwilling to open ourselves up to God is attachment. At the heart of love is connection. More than anything else in all the world, what we want most is connection. How we connect with our parents, ourselves, and our children is an area of psychology known as attachment theory. With a secure relationship with our parents, we can have a more secure ability to form healthy attachment relationships throughout our lives. We are also able to help our children learn healthy relationships of attachment and connection.

Sadly, when we have damaged, avoidant, or anxious relationships with our parents, that damaged style of connection is often unconsciously projected onto our relationship with God. Remote and distant parents who are uncaring often lead children to grow into adults who see God as remote, distant, and uncaring. Curt Thompson writes in his *Anatomy of the Soul* that "the attachment status of adults predicts with an *80 percent degree of confidence* the attachment pattern that their own children will develop toward them."[19] How we love our children will shape how they accept and find love in God. How we love others will also shape their attachment style toward God and others. Even those who face many adverse childhood experiences can find earned secure attachment in their adult years by being surrounded by loving relationships that they can trust.

With all the pain and hurt in the world, it might be hard for us to see God's love. Even the few people whom Jesus raised from the dead one day died again. Dorothy Linthicum and Janice Hicks, in their book *Redeeming Dementia*, remind us that "our tie with God does not depend entirely upon our own selves and minds, as Western individualistic culture is prone to think, but instead on the 'overflow' of God's reach to us."[20] We can find solid ground in God's love, even amid our human frailty. But it is okay to question and doubt from time to time where God's love is. In the face of horror, hardship, or societal sins, it is hard to find love. In our questioning, we think of ways that we may be God's love to the world. In our doubt, we can empathize with others who are also facing their own uncertainty. In our faith, we can be reminded that our hope lies in the world to come and that Christ has conquered death and sin.

The Neuroscience of Indifference

Many might define the opposite of love as fear. Rather than arguing what might be an exact opposite, this section will help detail the role of indifference as opposed to love. Later chapters go deeper into the role of fear in relation to anxiety and desperation. Many things can come into direct opposition with any individual fruit of the Spirit. What is important is that we understand how our systems have become hijacked and how to bring them back into relishing the way of love.

Where hate toward others might draw us into action, indifference causes us not to see or care about things going on in the world around us. To be indifferent can be so callous as to close off the heart and mind to the other in such a way that it almost does not exist. It is a horrifying reality that there are nearly a billion starving or undernourished people in the world; perhaps some who remain indifferent do not want to think about it because it can be overwhelming.[21] To consider or ruminate over all the many horrible things going on in the world is to take some personal responsibility for societal sin. Each of us is part of the wrongs of the world. To be too overwhelmed by ruminating over this can cause the stress response to go out of control. To let all the pain, hurt, and misery of the world to overwhelm us would be unbearable. It might cause us to freeze. However, without real lamentation at the injustice of the world, there is no room for love.

I believe it is because of our faith in God that we can bear the pain and suffering of the world. Rather than feeling overwhelmed, we can ask ourselves what we can do to make a difference. We can be reminded of the Great Commandment to love the Lord our God with all our mind, heart, and soul and to love our neighbor as ourselves. There are three parts to the commandment. We are to love God, love our neighbor, and retain love of ourselves. To be lost in ruminating on the pain and suffering of the world is not our call or our responsibility.

Martin Luther King Jr. once said, "The ultimate tragedy is not the oppression and cruelty by the bad people but the silence over that by the good people." Scripture reminds us that "those who say, 'I love God,' and hate their brothers or sisters, are liars; for those who do not love a brother or sister whom they have seen, cannot love God whom they have not seen'" (1 John 4:20). King also wrote in his "Letter from Birmingham Jail," "We are caught in an inescapable network of mutuality, tied in a single garment of destiny. Whatever affects one directly, affects all indirectly." Whether we choose to accept it or not, we are all intimately connected.

Though we are all intimately connected, we can choose indifference. As a neuroscientific example of how indifference can work, take a minute to feel what is going on in your hand. Hold it out in front of you without touching anything. If you take the time, you can feel individual joints, your fingernails, and even the little hairs on your skin. Much of the time, we are not consciously aware of these sensations because we do not take the time to examine them. It is the same with indifference. These sensations will not seem to exist unless we take the time to let them into our awareness. We can be indifferent to the many different signals coming from our hand into our brains just as we can be indifferent to the fact that there are children shooting other children in cities throughout our country. We can be indifferent to poverty, just like the joints of our hands. We can be indifferent to the feeling of our fingernails, just like we can be indifferent to the suffering of others. Or we can be full of love and empathy.

ALEXITHYMIA

Alexithymia is a condition marked by the inability to describe and relate to emotions. All of us suffer from it to varying degrees. I believe lamentation has a central role in Scripture to help us engage our emotions. Lamentation is feeling the sorrow of the world. Allowing yourself to feel passionately both grief and sorrow at the injustice and brokenness of the world is a building block of love. The meaning of the word *lamentation* in Latin signifies wailing and weeping. The more psychological distance we have from the pain of others, the less love we will experience.

In the 1960s, famous experiments by psychologist Stanley Milgram showed that when people were given greater amounts of psychological distance, they opted for allowing more pain to others farther removed from them. Dr. David Eagleman also found this in his research. Social rejection causes pain. When we see those we love experiencing pain, the pain matrix in our brains produces real pain for us. This pain can be productive as it enforces our drive toward connection.

The medial prefrontal cortex is involved in helping establish in-group and out-group. In his PBS series on the brain, Dr. Eagleman detailed that the medial prefrontal cortex is less active for many people when seeing photographs of the homeless because there is less connection to them.[22] The brain is shut off to their pain as if they have less existence or worth. This is the tragedy of indifference.

The humanity of the other is lost just as our own humanity is lost. Love is lost.

Understanding Our Emotions to Strengthen the Habit of Love

Empathy is at the heart of love. Unless we can relate to the feelings of others or our own feelings, we will not understand how to love others or ourselves. The anterior cingulate and the insula are highly involved in our process of emotions.

It is vital to teach our children how to identify and help regulate their emotions from the earliest of ages. We would not send mechanics into the world without first understanding how an engine works. Teaching children where the knee or toes are is as important as knowing how our parietal lobe works when we surrender to God's love and knowledge that all is of God. The brain is, in large part, the engine of the body. Why not give ourselves and our children the tools to access and shape it more effectively?

Psychotherapist Babette Rothschild is doing some of the most inspiring work to draw unconscious feelings into awareness. She studies the function of the body's autonomic nervous system (ANS), especially how it helps carry out commands sent to the body from the brain. The two main branches of the ANS are the parasympathetic and sympathetic nervous systems. They both play very active roles in our experience of emotion.

The parasympathetic nervous system (PNS) functions with our body's efforts to rest and digest. When we rest, more blood goes to our belly to digest food. We are more emotionally calm. A good metaphor is to think of it as our body's *brake* system. The sympathetic nervous system (SNS) is more involved in our body working to fight, take flight, or freeze under stress. It helps for a quick release of energy. It is more of an *accelerator* system. Activation of the SNS might increase heart rate, sweat, and muscle tone as the body readies to fight, though many of us are unaware of our own bodies responding in these ways.

Often, the work of either of the two main branches of the ANS is unconscious. Sadness, grief, or shame might draw us into a more lethargic state, such as the PNS working in low arousal. Muscles are slack, heart rate is lower, and breathing is shallower when the PNS is engaged. Emotions of rage, fear, anger, and excitement are much more associated with the sympathetic nervous system's fight and flight activation.[23] The amygdala and the body's stress response system are also involved in the SNS. By becoming more aware of our bodies, we become more aware of our emotional life and the life of the world. We also become more aware of how the fruit of the Spirit is working inside us or how bad fruit is working inside us.

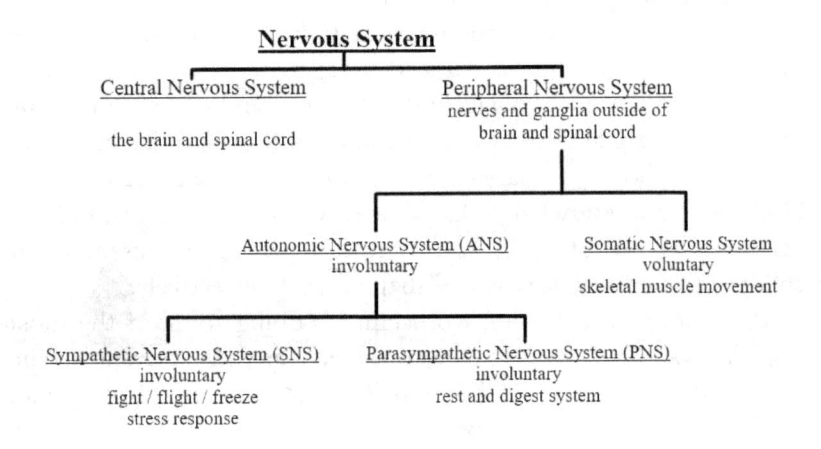

Nervous System
- **Central Nervous System** — the brain and spinal cord
- **Peripheral Nervous System** — nerves and ganglia outside of brain and spinal cord
  - **Autonomic Nervous System (ANS)** — involuntary
    - **Sympathetic Nervous System (SNS)** — involuntary; fight / flight / freeze; stress response
    - **Parasympathetic Nervous System (PNS)** — involuntary; rest and digest system
  - **Somatic Nervous System** — voluntary; skeletal muscle movement

Below are some common bodily reactions to our emotional states. These are very real processes that are at work within us. An emotion is not merely a mental concept, but a cascade of actions and reactions within us. The more that we are aware of our involuntary bodily processes, the more we can influence our reactivity.

Neuroscience and the FRUIT of the SPIRIT

Common Bodily Reactions of Emotional States

Awe	Shame	Peace
Feeling of connection, expansiveness, gratitude, curiosity, warmth, goosebumps, tears of wonder	Sick to the stomach, heaviness, pulled down, physical pain, feel like crying	Relaxed muscles, easy breathing, normal heart rate, rosy skin
Fear	**Mindfully Alert**	**Rage**
Fast heart rate, cold sweat, dry mouth, evacuate bowels, tense muscles, hyperventilation, only able to focus on object of fear	Access to frontal cortex, aware of body and sensations, warm hands, expansiveness, digestive system at work	Clenched fists, tense muscles, fast breathing, elevated heart rate, likely not able to access frontal cortex

Each emotional state comes with many different things. There is a sensation. Perhaps tightness, butterflies in the stomach, or blood boiling, to name a few. It might be connected with an image of a particular event or person. Maybe there are certain behaviors of others or certain of your own behaviors that draw out the emotion. What behaviors are playful? What behaviors are peaceful? What does the emotion mean to you?

Peter Levine's SIBAM method is an excellent tool to practice understanding how your emotions relate to your actions.[24] The SIBAM method takes into account five areas that create our emotional states and experience of the world. They are:

- Sensation
- Image
- Behavior
- Affect
- Meaning

As an example, let's take the behavior of watching the news.

> **Sensation**: tension in shoulders from stress, bewilderment and dizziness from being overwhelmed, feeling of being drawn into hatred or anger at an opposing side
>
> **Image**: carnage, trauma, death, political corruption
>
> **Behavior**: watching the news
>
> **Affect**: sadness, anger, despair, frustration
>
> **Overall Meaning**: Perhaps overall, there is a sense of wanting to connect with others by being informed. But with all the information in the world, why is there such a focus on the most horrible things? Overall, my time is better spent working for a church or nonprofit on actions to help my community and build true and lasting connection.

I invite you to contemplate what emotional states are of concern in your life. The example from my life was watching the news each day. I discovered that I was very anxious. My heart rate was up. I was tense. I had stress and tension in my back. After contemplating it for some time, I realized that underlying my desire for news was a desire to feel connected. I discovered that watching more news was not connecting me more to others but creating tension in my life. I decided with the help of others to limit my news diet to thirty minutes per week. My anxiety has gone down since that time, and my blood pressure decreased by ten points. I feel more connected to my family, friends, and work environment. It was because I looked at all the aspects of the emotional process that I was able to change. If you look at all the aspects of your emotions, how will you be able to change?

The Process of Emotional Experience

What we experience is embodied by thoughts, meaning, sensations, feelings, and images. Conscious reflection on feelings and behaviors will move your unconscious patterns into the light. Our mental and bodily states' awareness will help us gain control and form new neural character traits.

You could start small by picking just one behavior. The chart above of common bodily reactions to emotions can also help you get started. If you are having trouble, you could use music to help you get in touch with your feelings. Music is powerful in eliciting our feelings. Each of us has songs that connect to our joy or pain. You can use them to help you know how your body responds in feeling to these emotions.

Use the SIBAM categories to get at the heart of what you were feeling. Using the above resources will help build your empathy toward others and yourself. With more empathy, the walls inside and outside each of us will fall so that we will see the world more as *our* world rather than my world. This is similar to the Lord's Prayer, which reminds us: "Give us this day our daily bread" (Matthew 6:11).

When we take time to understand how we feel and process experiences, we can better love ourselves. We can also better understand how others feel so we can better love them. Through these practices, our neural circuits will change. Our capacity to love will grow. We will better love God.

Deeply listening to our bodies helps us better listen to the work of the Holy Spirit in us. Sometimes it is hard to feel and hear what God is calling us toward. We need to slow down and let the Holy Spirit speak to us through our bodies. Scripture reminds us, "The Spirit helps us in our weakness; for we do not know how to pray as we ought, but that very Spirit intercedes with sighs too deep for words" (Romans 8:26).

The SIBAM tool can help us find the deeper meaning behind what is going on in our bodies. It can be used for any experience of the fruit of the Spirit or of a bad fruit working in your life. Deep within our bodies, we often groan for the very things that are hard for us to receive. We groan for peace and joy. When we listen deeply to our bodies, then we can also find the source of the anxiety.

Looking deeply at the processes at work in our bodies will help us see the hidden chains that keep us bound. When we slow down, we can see the deeper meaning of why there is anxiety. We can also see how to overcome it. By looking deeply into ourselves, we can be healed like the blind man of Scripture. We can say to ourselves just as he said, "One thing I do know, that though I was blind, now I see" (John 9:25).

Think of one experience of a good fruit or bad fruit in your life, such as joy, addiction, peace, or anxiety. Break down the experience of the good or bad fruit below, sensing the various components.

Sensation	Image	Behavior	Affect	Meaning

Once you isolate the behavior of a bad or good fruit, you can start being more conscious of the feelings associated with it. You can also start seeing the meaning behind it. This will help you grow in that fruit or overcome a bad fruit. Take some time to linger on this tool each day, and it will change your life. When you have an intense feeling, take a step back and consider it as if you were doing research. You can examine your feelings and actions without being overcome by them. You can feel the emotion inside of you, such as anger or anxiety, without letting it define you. You can step back for a few minutes and consider what more might be going on. Some of the unconscious feelings or urges coursing through you can be overcome once you better understand their meaning.

For Group Discussion or Personal Reflection

Try this: Close your eyes and take a deep breath. Think of a time when you most felt God's love. If it is difficult to think of only one time, allow yourself to linger on the first example that came to mind. Do this for at least a minute, allowing yourself to relive the experience. Now, with your eyes still closed, turn your attention to how your body feels. Perhaps you feel a sense of lightness, connection, joy, peace, wonder, or awe. Perhaps you feel warmth. Where in your body do you feel these sensations? Describe below how it feels in your body to abide in God's love.

_____

_____

_____

Being more conscious of how it feels to abide in God's love will help you receive and surrender to it. The simple act of remembering God's love will bring the neurological wash of healing back over you so that you can return to it again and again. You can do this exercise at the end of each day, thinking of when you most felt God's love.

Keep these sensations in mind. Through what one habit will you let yourself go deeper to feel and relish God's love working in and through your body?

_____

_____

_____

Try this with caution. Do not retraumatize yourself. If a memory comes to mind that is too challenging, use a different memory. Close your eyes and take a deep breath. Think of a time when you most felt indifference from someone whose love you desperately desired. If it is difficult to think of only one time, allow yourself to linger on the first example that came to mind. Allow yourself to briefly relive the experience. After fifteen seconds and with your eyes still closed, turn your attention to how your body feels. Perhaps you feel a sense of anger, despair, muscles clenched, or knots in your stomach. Perhaps you feel like you're dizzy and spiraling downward. Describe below how it feels in your body to suffer from someone's indifference.

_____

_____

_____

Why even do an exercise to envision painful emotions? Being able to label and identify painful emotions and negative habits in our bodies helps us draw them into our consciousness so that we can overcome them. We are often unaware and unconscious of the processes going on in our bodies. We can become hijacked by trauma, habit, and addiction. To slow down and safely observe our painful emotions and negative habits will help us work through them. It can also help us teach others to do likewise.

What Scripture, resources, or tools from this book will help me overcome any of my own indifference toward others? Remember that Christ has called us to love our enemies.

_____

_____

What is one habitual tendency that is stuck in a cycle of indifference with my spouse, friends, family, or community? What specific changes would create more love?

What is a specific and measurable goal for me to create more of God's love that will help overcome an ingrained practice of indifference towards my organization, church, or political group?

Goal:

~ Pray ~

God, I am Yours. I say yes to love.
I will challenge and overcome my indifference.
I will lovingly invite others to overcome their indifference.
I surrender to your love.

Chapter 3 - Love vs. Indifference

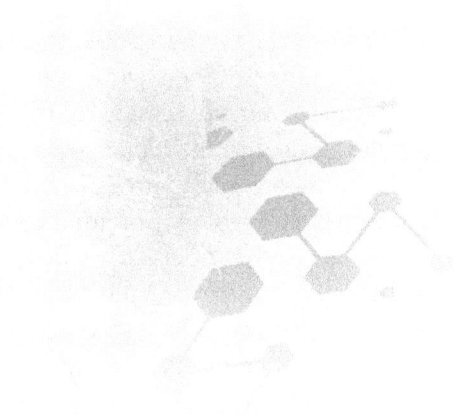

chapter four
Joy vs. Addiction

Joy is the serious business of heaven. ~ C.S. Lewis

Joy (Greek – Χαρα – *pronounced **kah**-rah*) might be defined as delight, gladness, or wonder. It need not be dependent on outward circumstances. Happiness is often associated with cause and effect. Happiness is often associated with receiving a reward. Our experience of joy, on the other hand, is a reward in itself.

The Habit of Joy

Earthly passions and desires are fleeting. Happiness is often defined by our relationship to outward experiences or circumstances. If I have piles of money in the bank, then I will be happy. If I have a fancy car, then I will feel secure. If I am famous, then I will be glamorous and happy. If I can just get hold of whatever it is, then I will finally be happy. The problem is that getting hold of something is only half of it. Once we get hold of anything, then we must keep it. Keeping hold of something fleeting is terribly difficult indeed. It is the paradox of addiction. Joy is beyond the happiness of resting in the security of outward experiences and circumstances. Joy is an end in itself.

The habit of joy deeply involves how we relate to any of the fruit of the Spirit working in us. When we surrender to God's work in us, then we can stop striving and trying to clutch onto success or failure. Surrendering to God's work in us is not limited to the fruit listed in Galatians. Fruit such as hospitality or humility are also areas where we can find joy. Having joy through hospitality is not judging ourselves or others by how many people we have served or how much enjoyment others have had through our efforts. Finding joy in hospitality is losing ourselves in doing our best. Our efforts can be a complete failure, but if we do our best, then we can find joy in being hospitable. No matter what fruit of the Spirit is working through us, when we lose ourselves to the utter joy of feeling and relishing God at work in us, then we can enjoy it no matter what the outcome.

We can find joy in humility by relishing a humble heart. We don't find joy in humility by judging whether we are the humblest or by constantly judging how humble we are compared to other people. Joy is about relationship and is very countercultural. Joy is an end in itself because God is with us always. If we surrender to God's love and joy, then it does not matter so much if we succeed in all our worldly pursuits or if we fail miserably. What matters is our relationship.

God yearns for us to use our skills to bring the fruit of the Spirit into the world. No matter what we accomplish, when we replace our will with God's will for us, then we can find joy. Viktor Frankl, who survived the Holocaust, wrote that if we have a *why* to live for, we can face any *how*.[25] Even in the darkest moments of the death camps, Frankl and others were able to find meaning and purpose despite their outward circumstances. No one could strip them of their connection with God.

Joy is closely related to grace, with both coming from the same word root. In Greek *grace* is χάρις (pronounced **chá**-ris). It is where we get the word charisma. Signs of God's grace working in us give us charisma. Any gift of the fruit of the Spirit working in us is the source of both our joy and grace. They are ends in themselves. Through God's Word, we know that we are to create fruit that will last, such as love, joy, peace, kindness, or gentleness. We live and dwell in God's love as we devote ourselves to serving God's will. With this *why* to live, we can face any *how*. We might fail miserably, and others might dash our hopes, but no one can take away God's grace and love for us and our efforts.

The Neuroscience of Joy

Much could be said about the neuroscience of joy. I would like to highlight four points: friendship, the flow state, laughter, and play.

FRIENDSHIP

For many of us, friendship is our greatest source of joy. What better friendship is there than that of our Lord? Christ has made the truth known to us and called us friends (John 15:15). Friendship with the Lord of life is our deepest resting place of joy. It is also our model for friendship with others here on earth. The baptismal vow of the Episcopal Church inspires us to seek and serve Christ in all persons and to love our neighbors as ourselves. It is through our relationship and friendship with Christ that we can see Christ in others. This sharing, partnership, and communion is at the heart of all our interactions and is known by the biblical word κοινωνία (Strong's #2842), pronounced koi-no-**nia**. *Koinonia* also translates as intimate fellowship. We both receive and offer the fruit of the Spirit with our friends through love, joy, peace, and kindness. There are expectations, but there is also understanding and compassion for failures and personal weaknesses.

Our mirror neurons are also central to our joy. When we act and intend for others to have joy, our mirror neurons fire allowing us to experience the same joy we hope others to have. When we perceive and expect Christ to work through others, it strengthens our sense of perception that Christ is indeed already at work not only in others but also in ourselves. The thalamus is a part of the brain that is a conduit of our sense perception. It is largely responsible for helping us feel that God is real in an objective sense. The more you strengthen an idea over and over, the more the thalamus helps the brain respond as if the idea is real within the world.

Everything can be perceived as intimate fellowship because all that we do is an expression of our relationship with God. As we share joy and wonder with God, we also share our failures and brokenness. Whether with our spouse, family members, close friends, or even our enemies, we can find joy because we act and intend knowing that God is already at work in us and through them. We can forgive our friends and enemies just as Christ forgives us. We can make room for and appreciate our differences. Christ has commanded us to love one another. Rather than seeing it as a burden or some rote rule to apply to every situation, we find joy in loving others even if they are our enemy because Christ is our example and our guiding light. It is about relationship and connection rather than simply outcomes and objectives.

Many of us are deeply lonely, and many of our relationships are fraught with brokenness and failure, but when we are true in our relationship with Christ, then all our relationships open up into profound joy because joy is at the center of all that we are. Our perception of all changes just as the thalamus will change. It is not how much we do, but our relationship of surrender and love. It is not if I love others perfectly, then God will love me. It is a surrender to God's love that is our wellspring to loving others. We are invited to say yes. No matter what failures come, our continual saying yes to God will continually keep us united in infinite joy.

FLOW

The Hungarian-American psychologist Mihaly Csikszentmihalyi has championed the idea of the flow state. It is also known as "being in the zone." Many people report losing a sense of time and space when they enter the flow state or "the zone." Like an artist or a painter in the midst of their creative expression, the flow state is when a person is totally absorbed in the process of using their skills. The same can be said for a teacher with students or a gardener in nature. Each of us has gifts that we share with the world that can become totally absorbing. We can enter the flow state when the challenge of a situation meets our skill to engage it. When our skills are being put to the test by a challenging situation, then we can get lost in it. It is the crossroads of creativity. If there is too much challenge in a situation, then we may feel overwhelmed by it. If we have few resources and the risk is high, then we might get filled with anxiety. If there is not enough challenge in a situation, it may seem boring. An example would be doing the exact same thing over and over again, year after year.

Any habit can help generate the flow state. What is so special about the creative flow state is that it is an end in itself. Being challenged to create and engage our skills within and among the world is the gift in itself. The same can be said of the fruit of the Spirit. As we grow in kindness, we will perhaps pick up on more social cues and learn of new ways to provide kindness to others. As we grow in patience, we can maintain our hopes and plans for the future, even amid the most difficult challenges. Because our creativity and the skills that we apply are to build God's kingdom, we need not get lost in measuring our productivity.

Our work toward building God's kingdom is not measured in who wins but in the very inclination to say yes to being a fellow worker. God rewards us with the riches of the flow state for our trying—win or lose. The notion of fellow worker comes up in Scripture, such as 1 Corinthians 3:9: "For we are God's servants, working together; you are God's field, God's building." The word translated as servants, (Strong's #4904) συνεργός, is also translated as colaborer or workfellow. As friends of the Lord of life, we are invited to be colaborers and workfellows in helping produce fruit that will last. We are invited to use our skills, to be challenged and to love our neighbors as ourselves. The charisma, grace, and talents that God gifts to us are refined and honed through our lives. God rewards us through the flow state when we give ourselves over to this invitation as colaborers, no matter how much we produce.

Howard Gardner, the Harvard psychologist, reminds us that the flow state is not simply for adults. Children also find creative ways that engage their skills and challenge so that their neural circuitry can develop early on. For a child, the act of producing a drawing for the refrigerator might be very challenging, but children are also rewarded by God in the flow state. Crayons stay within the lines, colors are chosen, flourishes are made, and the work of art is displayed prominently by magnets on the fridge for all to see! The same premise extends to an architect who creates a skyscraper or a composer who writes a symphony.

Below is a diagram illustrating how high skill and high challenge meet to generate the flow state.

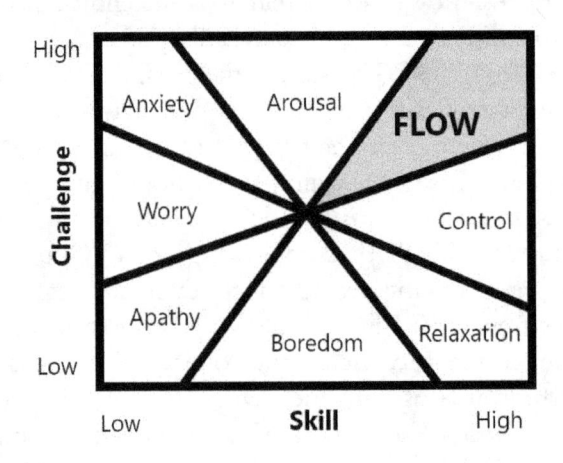

```
Challenge
High
    Anxiety    Arousal
                        FLOW
    Worry
                        Control
    Apathy
            Boredom    Relaxation
Low
    Low         Skill        High
```

The flow state swaps out conscious processing for more unconscious processing. Attention is heightened in the flow state. Areas of the brain that would inhibit quick thinking are turned off. Research has found that the dorsolateral prefrontal cortex, the area of the brain that involves self-monitoring, is turned off in the flow state. This allows for creativity to flow more freely. Research also shows that endorphins, norepinephrine, dopamine, anandamide, and serotonin play an active part in flow by stimulating pleasure and performance enhancement.[26]

Laughter

A universal gift wired into our beings is laughter. Laughter produces endorphins and an overall sense of well-being. It improves the immune system. It decreases stress hormones. It is wonderful! And we cannot get enough of it. Scripture reminds us to rejoice in it: "A glad heart makes a cheerful countenance, but by sorrow of heart the spirit is broken" (Proverbs 15:13).

In his book *Between Heaven and Mirth*, James Martin states that humor and laughter are at the heart of a spiritual life. The Dalai Lama and Archbishop Desmond Tutu also ruminate on its power in *The Book of Joy*. In the history of spiritual formation, it often was believed that heavy-handedness was the optimal approach. But now we recognize that people of faith live richer lives when they don't take themselves too seriously. With laughter, we can relish some of our most grieved mistakes or missteps. Is there a time in your life when you made an incredibly embarrassing mistake that you can now look back on and laugh? Laughter helps us overcome our drive toward perfection. We can embrace our imperfection and laugh at it!

PLAY

Children help us find joy. They are our greatest teachers about the joy of play. They help us to remember how important play is for us both spiritually and neurologically. The researcher Stuart Brown has made many discoveries about play. He has discovered how social play fires up the cerebellum, drives impulses to the frontal lobe and develops contextual memory. The cerebellum, once thought to be primarily for motor coordination, is now being seen as key to "cognitive functions such as attention, language processing, sensing musical rhythm, and more."[27] Play should not stop in childhood. Our lives should be infused with play throughout.

Play is enormously important in crafting the brain. If the purpose is more important than the act, it is probably not play. Even while doing seemingly mundane errands, we can be playful. We can be playful with the people we meet, marvel at the nature around us, or hum a tune while we are doing errands. Children find whimsy and delight so very easily and often in situations that might seem terribly boring to others. Not all of us have the luxury of a job that we absolutely love, but if we can find love and play while at work, we can also have joy. We can be playful with those we work with so that the work becomes play.

Play helps us remember that it is the act itself, not the product, which brings us joy. Even in difficult tasks and the challenges of life, we can remain playful. In their book *Play: How it Shapes the Brain, Opens the Imagination, and Invigorates the Soul*, Stuart Brown and Christopher Vaughan show that losing a sense of playfulness affects the ability to survive and thrive.

The Theology of Joy

The joy of the Lord is your strength. ~ Nehemiah 8:10

It is an immeasurable gift to have a resting place in God. Through God's assurance, we can surrender and find joy in a challenging and often disappointing world. The world is precarious and unstable. With God as our shepherd, we can experience everlasting joy. No matter how much we do, our world is unstable. It is only in relationship with an immutable, immeasurable, real God that there can be stability and joy.

I speak from the experience of my own life, of having no place to feel safe or secure. Even the most faithful and perfect spouse or partner will disappoint us at some point. Even the youngest and strongest person will someday die like the rest of us. Even the wealthiest people cannot stave off the ravages of time and death. Now that I have found God, I have the safety and security of knowing that I am in and with God. It might seem a strange thing to find joy through surrender. But when we give up our struggle to find happiness, joy is precisely what we can find.

When we replace our bad habits with the fruit of the Spirit, it does not matter so much what our successes and failures are. When we shift our focus toward love, then love will make a home in us. If we surrender to the call of God's love coursing through us and from us, then we can find joy. All we have to do is say yes and do our best. Our best will never be enough to overcome everything broken in the world, but we will know that we are enough. We can rest in the joy of knowing that God loves us. Jesus said, "Anyone who loves me will obey my teaching. My Father will love them, and we will come to them and make our home with them" (John 14:23).

Jesus did not say, anyone who is extremely successful I will love. He did not say, I won't love you unless you are the best.

Joy is our relationship of saying yes to God. Joy is a fruit of the Spirit, but it is also the disposition that we have to any fruit of the Spirit working in us. We can find joy in kindness. We can find joy in peace. We can find joy in gentleness. When we stop judging ourselves and others by their output and relish doing our best, then we can rest in joy. We can rest in the joy of God's love working through us, of God making a home in us. Christ helps remind us of this profound truth: "If you keep my commandments, you will abide in my love, just as I have kept my Father's commandments and abide in his love. I have said these things to you so that my joy may be in you, and that your joy may be complete" (John 15:10–11).

The Neuroscience of Addiction

You are slaves of the one whom you obey. ~ Romans 6:16

Sadness is often considered the opposite of joy. I believe addiction is in many ways the opposite of joy, largely because of how it functions neurologically. Joy is a reward in itself, but its opposite is truly opposite. Addiction craves external rewards and numbs us to the joy of actually experiencing them. Addiction is not reward in itself. It does not provide either love or creativity. The thrill comes from the chase. It is a hedonic treadmill. Addiction is defined by abuse, dependence, and pathological craving.

The neurochemical dopamine is at the heart of the reward system. Healthy levels of dopamine will help us with motivation and in the pursuit of desires. It is vitally important to us. Dopamine is released from the nucleus accumbens and ventral tegmentum area. In the frontal cortex, it will help us work toward our desired goals. It will also help with decision-making. Dopamine will help us feel rewarded in our pursuit of meaning and purpose.

If the meaning and purpose we find in life is hurtful to others or found through addiction, then the dopamine circuit gets turned toward the negative. Studies have shown that elevated levels of dopamine do not make people more content. Rather they are geared up for wanting more. They become addicts. If you have not

Chapter 4 - Joy vs. Addiction

personally suffered from addiction, it is almost certain that you know someone who does or has suffered.

Addiction can be for substances such as alcohol as well as in behaviors. Behavioral addiction can range from food, pornography, video games, gambling, shopping, or even exercise. It can be for many things. Much of our sensationalized, traumatic news can fit into the category of addiction such as the violence we see on television and in video games. The increased prevalence and entertainment of violence has been labeled by some as the pornography of violence.

Common to various types of addiction is the hijacking of the reward system. Numbing of the reward, tolerance, a large release of dopamine, and a weakened prefrontal cortex inhibitory response are all features of addiction and the hijack of our reward system. When we suffer from addiction, the reward actually becomes less appealing over time. Addicts need a bigger risk and reward to maintain a sense of desire and stimulation. When overstimulated, the nucleus accumbens through a binding protein known as CREB (cAMP response element-binding protein), activates the release of dynorphin. Dynorphin inhibits overstimulation of the nucleus accumbens.[28] What happens with addiction is that over time, the feeling of pleasure decreases just as craving increases, because the brain is naturally trying to limit overstimulation. Neuroscience teaches us that more will become less.

Addiction is much more than a pleasurable diversion. In addiction, there is an inability to stop. Addiction is destructive to our lives and relationships. When our dopamine system is out of control, it is more like scratching an itch rather than medicine for a wound. Many of our desires are very basic, such as for food or for procreation. Advertisers know to play on these desires. Advertisers also play on our fears, pride, and feelings of in-group and out-group. They often try to create our desires for us. Cues are a large part of addiction. Shiny, fast, and big are just a few that we could name. When our goals get manipulated, then we can become addicts. Elevated dopamine will drive us toward craving.

Some of the most addictive substances, like cocaine or methamphetamine, ramp up the effect of dopamine. The problem

Neuroscience and the FRUIT of the SPIRIT

is that these systems of ramping up get so out of whack that they need more and more of the drug to produce the desired effect. Much of our society is stuck in cycles of addiction: release, fear, guilt, tension, release, fear, guilt, tension. The dopamine reward circuit must not get hijacked by fear.

Society can train people to fear rejection by telling them that they are part of an out-group. They are told that they need the reward of being accepted or of being part of the in-group. In school, this could be the pressure to wear certain clothes, act in a certain way, or think like others. Thus, the cycle of addiction is born. What is so tragic is that it is often unconscious. We often do things because we are told or taught them by others. Others tell us or teach us without knowing they are teaching or telling us. Many of us have a genetic predisposition toward addiction as well.

Our possessions can come to possess us. Our striving to get things only leaves us with the fear of them being taken away. It might also leave us suspicious of others. Research has shown that lottery winners are actually less content than before they won. With more stress, people vying for their money, and poor decision-making, lottery winners often confess to being happier before the winnings.

Some of the most "successful" people are often those with a type A personality. The type A personality is defined by constant striving, impatience, and competitiveness. Another term for describing the type A personality is joyless striving. Those who have the most sometimes can't appreciate any of what they have because they are so possessed by wanting more. Another psychological term for the disease of not being able to appreciate overabundance is affluenza.

One might argue that many have become addicted to hate. Does it not sometimes seem that there is abuse, dependence, and pathological craving toward hating people of opposing political parties? Perhaps even more troubling is our country's addiction to debt. At over twenty-six trillion dollars and climbing, there still seems almost unanimous consensus among politicians to ignore the problem. Not recognizing our problems is also a key feature of addiction. Our children and grandchildren are shackled to the sins of today. What legacy are we going to leave them? And what will they think of us when they reach adulthood?

Strengthening the Habit of Joy: The Butterfly Effect

Earlier in this book, I described the Butterfly Effect, discovered by the scientist Edward Lorenz while computing weather models. He found that the slightest difference in an initial query ultimately produced extremely different weather patterns when running simulations. Each one of us, no matter how small we seem in our own minds, is infinitely powerful. Our lives change the world.

To think of our lives as a metaphor of a butterfly might seem extremely contrary to what one might expect or hope. It might seem ridiculous. A butterfly is a tiny insect with a brief life, but it is a rich reminder that our lives are both very small and brief as well. When seen against the fabric of time and space, each human is so very small. But like the butterfly, each of us is infinitely intertwined with all things and has infinite impact. Being vulnerable and embracing the fact that we are finite is a way that we can also embrace infinity. Those who confront death face-to-face often are the most alive among us. Those who deny the reality of death also deny life because they are unable to truly appreciate the preciousness of every moment.

The universe and all the competing signals of culture and society swirling around us can seem overwhelming, like a hurricane. We will be fully alive when we are honest with ourselves about how very small we are. Then God's brilliance can shine through us.

When we allow the fruit of the Spirit to work through us, then from our innermost being will burst forth torrents, floods, and rivers of living water (John 7:38). All of us can connect with the power of nature. All of us have seen the massive power of a thunderstorm. We have seen lightning flash across the sky. Jesus uses this imagery of torrents and rivers bursting to describe the change that happens in us through our faith. It is so powerful because it speaks to the power of the Holy Spirit coursing in and through us.

The imagery of the Butterfly Effect is connected to weather patterns. However small we may feel, when we allow the Holy Spirit to work through us in love, joy, and peace, then God's glory bursts forth from us like a mighty river. Like the beating wings of a butterfly, the works that we do might seem small, but they cause enormous ripple effects that span out into eternity.

Like the brilliance of a butterfly's coloring, the light that shines through us out into the world also captivates others with the eternal. A butterfly is mysterious and beautiful. The markings, luminescent and intricate, are all so extravagant. Each human is infinitely unique in a similar way. Seeing the infinitely unique beauty of each of us helps us see the infinitely unique beauty of every moment. Everything is pregnant with that eternity. Everything is intertwined.

Research shows that we are more joyful, have higher levels of self-esteem and concentration, and have more flow when we are creative and active.[29] Replacing our will with God's will for us is the source of our joy. Christ said, "If you keep my commands, you will remain in my love, just as I have kept my Father's commands and remain in his love. I have told you this so that my joy may be in you and that your joy may be complete" (John 15:10–11). Following God's will is the source of our joy.

For Group Discussion or Personal Reflection

Try this: Close your eyes and take a deep breath. Think of a time when you most felt God's joy. If it is difficult to think of only one time, allow yourself to linger on the first example that came to mind. Do this for at least a minute, allowing yourself to relive the experience. Now with your eyes still closed, turn your attention to how your body feels. Perhaps you feel a sense of lightness, playfulness, laughter, or awe. Perhaps you feel tingles on your skin. Where in your body do you feel these sensations? Describe below how it feels in your body to abide in God's joy.

_____

_____

_____

You can do this exercise at the end of each day, thinking of when you most felt God's joy the previous day.

Keeping these sensations in mind, through what one habit will you let yourself go deeper to feel and relish God's joy working in and through your body?

_____

_____

_____

Try this with caution. Do not retraumatize yourself. If a memory comes to mind that is too challenging, use a different memory: Close your eyes and take a deep breath. Think of a time when you struggled with addiction. If it is difficult to think of only one time, allow yourself to linger the first example that came to mind. Allow yourself to briefly relive the experience. After fifteen seconds and with your eyes still closed, turn your attention to how your body feels. Perhaps you feel a sense of despair or hopelessness. Your muscles may be clenched, or you may have knots in your stomach. You might feel out of control. Describe below how it feels in your body to suffer from addiction.

_____

_____

_____

What is one source of my craving or addiction? What Scripture, resources, or tools from this book will help me overcome it?

_____

_____

_____

What one habit or settled tendency is stuck in a cycle of craving and addiction with my spouse, friends, family, or community? What specific changes would create more joy?

_____

_____

_____

What is one specific and measurable goal to create more of God's joy to help overcome an ingrained culture of addiction at my organization, church, or political group?

Goal:
_____

_____

_____

~ Pray ~

God, I am Yours. I say yes to joy.
I will challenge and overcome my craving and addiction.
I surrender to Your joy.

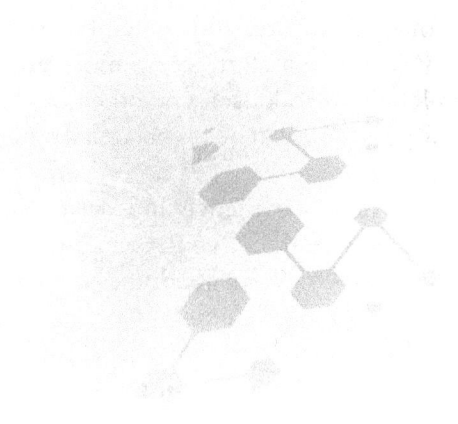

chapter five
Peace vs. Anxiety

> Come to me, all you that are weary and are carrying heavy burdens, and I will give you rest. ~ Matthew 11:28

Peace (Greek – Ειρηνη – *pronounced eh-**rey**-ney*): It is often understood as harmony, concord, security, safety, prosperity, or felicity. It can also mean quietness or stillness. In Hebrew, the word for peace is *shalom* (שָׁלוֹם). It is often associated with a greeting of hello or goodbye, but the term is much deeper. It can mean peace and harmony, but it also means wholeness and completeness. Theologically, it can have a deeper significance. It means to be enough.

The Habit of Peace

Many of us are overwhelmed by the responsibilities and challenges of our lives. Perhaps it is difficult to have time set apart to just relish. Even if it is for three to five minutes, stopping and being able to reflect on the blessings of your life has a huge impact. If we can stop, even briefly, every day for a short time and remember our blessings, then the habit can stick. We can start seeing more and more blessings around us. It will help us to loosen up and enjoy. It can often be difficult to let in the good. We can be preoccupied with all the things we feel obligated to do.

Peace involves allowing ourselves to experience and be in the present moment. Walking, standing, breathing, and seeing are all incredibly beautiful gifts. To relish and enjoy the goodness of life is a treasure. Every moment is loaded with opportunity.

Relishing God's goodness also involves resting in it. Christ invites us, "Come to me, all you that are weary and are carrying heavy burdens, and I will give you rest" (Matthew 11:28). The Greek word used for come (δεῦτε) also means follow according to *Strong's Concordance*.[30] We are not simply invited to someplace where we can hide from strife. It would be nice to have a cozy place away from everything where we could be safe.

It is in following Christ that we find safety, not from hiding from the hardships of the world. Oswald Chambers describes this movement very similarly: "Once I press myself into action, I immediately begin to live. Anything less is merely existing. The moments I truly live are the moments when I act with my entire will . . . His word 'come' means to 'act.'"[31] Rather than seeing rest as a removal from strife and hardship, we can see rest in our overall disposition. We can relish our call to serve God in all that we do and all who we are. No matter if we succeed or fail, we can relish and rest in our communion with God through the conviction in our hearts in serving the way of love. This is an active movement but does not have to be frenetic.

Being calm in our skin and being content with ourselves are active movements. While it seems that there is a hurricane of tragedy going on around us in the world, if our heart is centered in Christ's love, then we can face the tragedy of the world in peace. We can rest in Christ's presence and invite others to rest in it as well. We can invite them to be comfortable within their skin. We can invite them to relish God's goodness. This is not striving, though it is most certainly active. It is a goodness that is so rich and wonderful that it speaks for itself.

When our disposition is toward relishing the good and resting in God's peace, then it naturally draws others toward it. It is an invitation by itself. When others see and experience our peace, they are naturally drawn to it and naturally drawn to us. They see in us what they desire most for themselves. This is a rest and peace that we all hope and yearn for.

The Theology of Peace

To live in peace is to live in the knowledge that we are enough. We are enough because we are created in the image of God. Research has shown that when children are "encouraged to believe that their bad grades come from lack of effort rather than lack of intelligence, they show remarkable gains in both persistence and accomplishment."[32] When we are told that we are valuable rather than intrinsically stupid, then we can grow.

God declares of all of us that we are beautifully and wonderfully made. Those of us with chronic illness might struggle more with this declaration, but it is true nonetheless. Each one of us is enough. We are invited by God to see our perfection, even in our imperfection. We can never be everything. We can never have everything. To chase after perfection is an illness. Outside of God, where is peace? Peace is fleeting outside of God.

The Neuroscience of Peace

While there are many ways to think about our peace, harmony, and feeling of wholeness, I would like to concentrate on three.

MINDFULNESS AND MEDITATION

Being enough is about accepting ourselves and being present in the moment. There has been much research on mindfulness in past years. Mindfulness is the ability to bring your attention to the present. It is often associated with being calm within our skin. It involves being conscious and aware.

Research has shown that meditation helps strengthen the default mode network (DMN). The DMN involves many areas of the brain, as well as their interconnectivity. When the mind wanders, we might excessively ruminate over past problems, have anxiety about the future, or daydream about some fantasy rather than engage reality. Our mind will jump around like a monkey unless we can train it. One way of training the mind is by relishing the good in our lives. Reflecting on the good for at least thirty seconds will build and strengthen the neural pathway. Neurons that fire together wire together. When we are calm, our cortisol level will go down. Other signs of being calm are relaxed and toned muscles, warm hands and feet, and accessibility to the frontal cortex. Being present rather than ruminating over past failures or anxiety of the future is a foundation of peace. Being mindful draws us into the present.

Some Christians are quite apprehensive about meditation because it is associated with Buddhism. The Bible is full of references to meditation. One example is: "Let the words of my mouth and the meditation of my heart be acceptable to you, O Lord, my rock and my redeemer" (Psalm 19:14). Psalm 1:1–2 is also a good example: "Happy are those who do not follow the advice of the wicked, or take the path that sinners tread, or sit in the seat of scoffers; but their delight is in the law of the Lord, and on his law they meditate day and night."

When we dedicate our minds and our lives to meditating on God's Word, we internalize and strengthen our neural pathways that remind us of God's presence in the world. The thalamus relays information that comes into our brains. It also overlays information onto the information we receive by interpreting it one way or another. Our minds include both conscious, working memory and unconscious, implicit memory. We may not be consciously aware of all the ways that we interpret and remember our reality, but the more we infuse every moment, thought, and action toward God's presence and God's Word, the more that reality will live within us.

In psychology, there is a concept known as priming. Priming is our brain's way of wiring unconscious influence toward specific responses. Continued reflection and relishing of God's goodness will prime us to unconsciously expect and observe God's goodness at work. The process works in the negative as well. We can be unconsciously drawn toward the negative when we perpetually dwell on and accept the negative. Constant meditation on God's loving presence will change our being. One of the best reminders of this is Psalm 46:10: "Be still and know that I am God."

There are so many distractions and invitations pulling our minds one way or another. Many of the distractions are not good for us at all. Stilling our minds will still our bodies so that we can become vessels of God's goodness. We can retrain our focus so that our holiness is both conscious and unconscious. When our working memory is aware of God's presence working in and through our bodies and minds, we are deeply blessed, for "Blessed are the pure in heart, for they will see God" (Matthew 5:8). Not only will we see God, but we will feel God's loving presence in us and with us.

There are many ways to meditate. We do not have to be Buddhist to practice meditation, but we can learn much from Eastern styles of meditation and enjoy the benefits of practicing them. These include concentration on the breath and body awareness.

Meditation on compassion and the love of God has been shown to provide increased gamma brain waves. This has been found in Carmelite nuns as well as Buddhist monks.[33] The four main types of brain wave patterns, from lowest to highest frequency, are delta, theta, alpha, and beta. Delta waves are most present during sleep and theta more so when we are drowsy. Alpha waves are present during relaxed thought, such as daydreaming. Beta waves can be seen when the brain is alert and concentrated. Gamma waves are the highest frequency brain waves and are generally very shortly sustained in most minds. Perhaps from a sudden insight or through the realization of a taste of a favorite food, there will be spikes in gamma waves. Research shows that mindfulness and meditation, especially on compassion, can alter our mind's trait to be more enveloped by gamma waves. Those who experience more gamma brain waves report feeling more "vastness in their experience as if all their senses were wide open to the full, rich panorama of experience."[34]

Another way that mindfulness and meditation bring harmony to our bodies is through the insula. The insula is a part of the brain that helps bring awareness about our bodily organs. If we become mindful of our bodies and organs through meditation, then our bodies will be more integrated with our brains. You can be better aware of an increased heart rate, tightness in your shoulders, or other responses from your reactions. More awareness will give you greater peace and harmony with yourself and your environment. Research has shown that "higher insula activation is associated with greater awareness not only of physical sensations but also of emotions." [35] Because our emotions come with real physical sensations, it is no wonder that when we have a better awareness of our physical sensations, we will have a better awareness of our emotions.

Centering Prayer is a popular and powerful form of Christian meditation. It is an exceptional tool to help find and strengthen our connection to God's presence. [36] The parietal-frontal circuit, described earlier in the book, helps establish a relationship between our conceptions of self and God. It helps establish the feeling of God's presence in time and space, as well as our connection to this reality. The more we meditate on God's presence, the more it becomes real.

To practice Centering Prayer, find resources at www.contemplativeoutreach.org. A simplified version is below:

1) Sit comfortably with eyes closed. Relax and let yourself be quiet. Revel in God's love and presence surrounding you.
2) Choose a sacred word, phrase, or passage from Scripture that helps you remember God's love and presence with you. Let the phrase or Scripture be present to you.
3) If you find that you are distracted, simply return to the word, phrase, or Scripture.
4) Whenever you are aware of any other thoughts, feelings, or images, simply return to your word or phrase that anchors you to God's love.
5) Practice the above for twenty minutes per day. You can set a gentle alarm timer to help yourself know your time.

Centering Prayer is not meant to simply be a twenty-minute exercise, but a time to reframe our minds so that every moment of our lives, we can invite and dwell in God's presence. The more you practice Centering Prayer, the more you will feel God working in and through you, and the more you will prime yourself to receive God's riches that are hardwired into your being.

REST

The tranquility of good sleep is something that should not be underrated. Neither should we forget that naps and relaxation time are crucial to our well-being. These are things that primarily recharge and are vitally important to us. However, I would like to concentrate on another aspect of rest that relates to peace. True rest is relationship with God. When we can rest in an indwelling of the Holy Spirit, then we will grow in peace. It is not about doing more or judging ourselves and others by how productive we are. Rest is about dwelling in a state of right being. It is about relishing and embracing the way that we are neurologically hardwired. Craving, addiction, anxiety, and all the other bad fruit that can habitually overrun our neurological makeup will strip us of God's peace. When we live a life in and by all the fruit of the Spirit, then we can live in peace.

The neuroscientific basis of this is illustrated in many ways throughout these pages. This book has many tools, resources, and means to help strengthen your relationship with God, but it is not helpful to get caught up in more busyness by them. There are many excellent tools out there. Richard Foster's *Celebration of Discipline* has fantastic tools. Bishop Michael Curry's "The Way of Love" initiative has many practices that will draw us deeper into relationship with God.[37] No matter where we find tools to bring us closer to God, we can remember that it is about relationship and grace. As our lives become more and more an expression of the fruit of the Spirit through love, joy, and peace, we will become more at home in ourselves. We can rest in this relationship. We can choose God's grace. We can avoid busyness and the tyranny of the urgent. We can have peace.

AWE

The amount of awe and wonder we have in our lives is largely proportional to our ability to be present and find peace. Awe has amazing neurological effects for us. It draws the mind to a greater sense of self, helps us think more creatively, is positive for our health, and draws us to be more collaborative and social.[38] Even the simplistic beauty of a blade of grass can draw us into awe at the wonder of creation. Wonder is feeling excited by an unexpected encounter where beauty, truth, or a greater sense of reality is found.[39]

We could all use more awe and wonder. Awe and wonder are present in our bodies and in the vastness of space. Children often teach me much about awe and wonder. Children find them in the simplest of things. If we could find more awe and wonder in simple things as children do, we would be so much richer! Where do you find wonder and awe in your life? Where could you find more?

The Neuroscience of Anxiety

The word anxiety comes from the Latin *angere*, meaning to choke or to squeeze. Strangely, that is exactly what can happen in our brains when we feel under threat or danger. When we are relaxed and calm, more blood will go to the prefrontal cortex. When our emotional response is disproportionate to the stimulus, this process is called an amygdala hijack. The amygdala is responsible for the detection and response to threats. Fear triggers the amygdala to send a distress signal to the hypothalamus. In fear or anger, the hypothalamus sends corticotropin-releasing factor to the pituitary gland. The pituitary then sends adrenocorticotropic hormones to the adrenal glands to release adrenaline and cortisol, the stress hormone. Cortisol is a glucocorticoid hormone. It functions to metabolize fat, protein, and carbohydrates to quickly put us in survival mode. The stress response allows for energy to be converted quickly. The hypothalamus, pituitary, and adrenal glands make up this axis (the HPA axis).

When you are stressed, think about what is going on in your body. Your blood pressure goes up, heart rate increases and glucose is dumped into your system. In fear, we get ready to fight or take flight. Through excessive fear and anxiety, we can also freeze.

If our default mode network (DMN) is not trained toward concentrating on the present and being consciously aware, then our minds might move toward ruminating over the past or on the anxiety of the future. We might regret or feel fearful about what we have done in the past. We might gear up toward a fight or flight from some future activity. In our anxiety, we will choke ourselves off from peace. Children who are not taught by parents how to reframe and train their minds to return to a DMN of resilience may have much more difficulty throughout life when faced with stressful situations.

Even with the best teaching and nurturing from parents, traumatic situations can damage our systems of governing the stress response. Through intense or prolonged traumatization, the ability to recognize or recover from threats can decrease. We can even train our bodies to expect and be drawn toward trauma and increased anxiety. To watch traumatic news day after day can be traumatizing. Even more damaging is when traumatic news becomes sensationalized as if it is entertainment.

Intense anxiety over a long period can also damage the hippocampus. The hippocampus helps the nervous system become calm. Victims of trauma and abuse have been found to have shrunken hippocampi. Through chronic stress, the hippocampus might become so affected that we can become confused about our own memories of what is real or unreal.[40]

Villainizing fear and anxiety is not the best course. Our amygdala gives us the ability to survive. Unless we can label and recognize threats in the world, we would have no way to survive. Knowing and labeling our fears can also have tremendous value in our healing. Unless we understand and appreciate our most beloved treasures, as well as the weight of what it would be to lose them, we are not able to navigate the risks and opportunities of life.

Our Scripture reminds us, "There is no fear in love, but perfect love casts out fear; for fear has to do with punishment, and whoever fears has not reached perfection in love" (1 John 4:18). The word used in Greek here is φόβος, pronounced **pho**-bos, meaning dread or terror. It is where we get the word phobia. After we survive threats and attacks, we can remember fearful situations. We can hold in mind our fear but not be overwhelmed by it. We can calmly contextualize our fearful memories through our executive function rather than being overwhelmed in the body's fear response. In terror or extreme anxiety, we become overwhelmed by fear. There is no terror or sense of punishment in love. Holding our memories of fearful situations in mind while taking risks to walk in the way of love gives us even more appreciation for how precious love is.

Strengthening the Habit of Peace

Anthony de Mello, in his book *Sadhana,* has an excellent tool for taking in the good of our lives. Often, when we have a peak experience, a moment of intense exhilaration, or excitement, we are too busy to let ourselves truly appreciate it. Each of us has moments in our lives when there has been something awe-inspiring. Even if fleeting, these moments are profound and live with us. The goal of this exercise is to return to those moments in our minds. I invite you now to try this exercise.

Picture in your mind and heart a time when you felt peace and joy. Where are you? Who are you with? What is happening? Take time to remember the details that gave you this joy. What was your overall sense? Stay with the scene. Where was God for you in this scene? What was God doing? What was God's gift?

After you have stayed with the scene and reveled in the joy and peace, take a moment to give God thanks for it. The habit of returning to moments of profound peace and joy will help us remember and feel more deeply the peace and joy in every moment. There is extraordinary peace in experiencing the wonder of what many would find simply ordinary. Reveling in peace will also help us feel God's presence. Even five minutes of peace, reveling in the joy of fresh air and sunshine, is a marvelous thing. We can find peace in the majesty of even something as simple as a blade of grass. God has given us so much to be grateful for. Even we who have lived with chronic pain have much to revel in. These are treasures in our minds and hearts to return to and cherish. The more we return to the gifts of our life, the more the habit of peace will grow. The habit of taking in and relishing the good of life will also grow. We can rest in goodness. We can find rest in the wonder and knowledge of the majesty and blessings of God.

In chapter 9 of this book, you will find the Daily Examen prayer. It will help you focus and relish on God's gifts in your life each day.

Neuroscience and the FRUIT of the SPIRIT

It is an excellent tool to build the habit and neural pathways to relish the peace and goodness of your life more fully.

For Group Discussion or Personal Reflection

Try this: Close your eyes and take a deep breath. Think of a time when you most felt God's peace. If it is difficult to think of only one time, allow yourself to linger on the first example that came to mind. Do this for at least a minute, allowing yourself to relive the experience. Now with your eyes still closed, turn your attention to how your body feels. Perhaps you feel a sense of calm, tranquility, or safety wash over you. Perhaps you feel embraced in God's protection. Where in your body do you feel these sensations? Describe below how it feels in your body to abide in God's peace.

_____

_____

_____

You can do this exercise at the end of each day, thinking of the time during the day when you most felt God's peace.

Keeping these sensations in mind, what one habit will you deepen to feel and relish God's peace working in and through your body?

_____

_____

_____

Try this with caution. Do not retraumatize yourself. If a memory comes to mind that is too challenging, use a different memory. Close your eyes and take a deep breath. Think of a time when you felt anxious. If it is difficult to think of only one time, allow yourself to linger on the first example that came to mind. Allow yourself to relive the experience briefly. After fifteen seconds and with your eyes still closed, turn your attention to how your body feels. Perhaps you feel a sense of agitation, dread, restlessness, worry, nausea, or dizziness. Describe below how it feels in your body to feel anxious.

_____

_____

_____

What is one source of my anxiety? What Scripture, resources, or tools from this book will help me overcome it?

_____

_____

_____

What one habit or settled tendency is stuck in a cycle of anxiety with my spouse, friends, family, or community? What specific changes would create more systemic peace?

_____

_____

_____

What is one specific and measurable goal to create more of God's peace that will help overcome an ingrained practice of anxiety at my organization, church, or political group?

Goal:

_____

_____

_____

~ Pray ~

God, I am Yours. I say yes to peace.
I will challenge and overcome my anxiety.
I surrender to Your peace. I am enough.

chapter six
Patience vs. Desperation

And we want each one of you to show the same diligence so as to realize the full assurance of hope to the very end, so that you may not become sluggish, but imitators of those who through faith and patience inherit the promises. ~ Hebrews 6:11–12

I wait for the Lord, my soul waits, and in his word I hope; my soul waits for the Lord more than those who watch for the morning. ~ Psalm 130:5–6

Patience (Greek – μακροθυμια – *pronounced mah-krow-**thew**-me-ah*): The word in Greek combines μακρός (pronounced *makros*), meaning long, with θυμός (pronounced *thumos*), meaning anger or an outburst of passion. A transliteral definition would be slow to anger. Patience also includes the qualities of endurance, steadfastness, perseverance, forbearance, and longsuffering. It involves bearing annoyance or misfortune without an immediate desire for revenge. In Spanish, the word *esperar* means both to hope and to wait. Patience also involves both hoping and waiting.

The Habit of Patience

Being patient involves maintaining self-control despite our circumstances. It involves maintaining love and forgiveness even under challenging situations. Patience has much to do with not letting ourselves be overcome by anger or fear. Patience is how we maintain our faith in the face of adversity. When we have the impulse to respond in anger and judgment but instead refrain, this is patience at work. Being patient in adversity helps us break the cycle of revenge. Jesus said that by the same standard we judge, so too will we be judged. The example of the men judging the woman who had committed adultery reveals how each of us has the power to throw a stone. If we do not practice patience, we will all end up throwing stones at each other. Sometimes that is exactly how it feels in today's day and age.

When we think of patience, we also generally think of being patient in relationship to a specific result or desire. We can wait patiently for a loved one to return. We can be patient in the fulfillment of a goal. Being patient is a way of life, but it ought not to be completely separated from our goals and desires. To be patient without any ultimate goals in mind is to be idle. Remaining tranquil and unmoved even amid our hopes and dreams being dashed can be submission and capitulation. Letting others act in evil ways without challenging them is enabling. Patience calls us to respond in love rather than retaliation. Laziness and sloth are generally considered sinful. It is with purpose that our hopes and longsuffering become powerful. Waiting is part and parcel with hope. Scripture reminds us to wait on the Lord. Our hopes, dreams, and prayers will be challenged in many ways, but we can retain hope. We can respond in love rather than continue the cycle of revenge. Challenges may cause us to modify what we hope for and how we respond, but our hope and response of love can remain lest we fall into despair or hatred.

The Neuroscience of Patience

The engineering definition of resilience is quite helpful in clarifying its meaning. Resilience is the ability to absorb or release tension without fracture or distortion. When we crack, we can become irritable or even hateful rather than keep our composure and steadfastness. We can also fall into complete hopelessness. In their book, *The Emotional Life of Your Brain*, Richard Davidson and Sharon Begley show that increased neuronal connections between the prefrontal cortex and the amygdala help us bounce back from adversity.[41] This is because the prefrontal cortex can help dampen fear or anger being processed in the amygdala. The stronger conception of self and executive function you have, the more you can overcome fear and anger-inducing distraction. The more goal-oriented mindset you have, the stronger your resilience.

When we are able to feel safe and calm, the autonomic system operates through the integration of the ventral vagus branch of the vagus nerve. We have relaxed muscles, can be social and engage others, blood flows to the skin, and are capable of pleasurable emotions. We have access to our prefrontal cortex when we feel safe and calm.

The prefrontal cortex has distinct areas with distinct roles. The dorsolateral prefrontal cortex (DLPFC) is an area involved in planning and goal setting. Additionally, the orbitofrontal cortex (OFC) helps inhibit impulsive and emotional reaction in coordination with the anterior cingulate cortex (ACC). There is much research available that demonstrates that what we pay attention to will determine how our brain structures and restructures. Remember Hebb's Law: neurons that fire together wire together. The prefrontal cortex, where executive function largely resides, helps override the emotional centers of the brain such as the amygdala.

Visualizing our goals, taking time to breathe, filtering out distractions, and controlling our anxiety are all ways that our brain will wire to watch and wait for our goals and desires. The more practice we make at enduring the longsuffering of waiting and watching for our goals, the stronger our neural connections of patience will become. It might seem strange to attach goal setting with patience. But neurologically speaking, what we wait and watch for helps us focus on overcoming the amygdala's perception of threats, dangers, and worries that might derail our prefrontal cortex. If we are unable to watch and wait, we will instead act on impulse and anxiety. Our Lord reminds us that those who seek shall find (Matthew 7:7). This encourages us to wait and hope. Despite any setbacks or failures, we can maintain our hope.

Responding in love rather than retaliation also strengthens the anterior cingulate cortex. Responding with hate or worry will diminish the strength of our circuitry that draws us toward love. Because we are wired for love, we are wired to respond without revenge. When we look at history, we can easily see that revenge never ultimately is the best option.

The Theology of Patience

When we are patient, we maintain our hope, expectation, and anticipation despite setbacks and failures. God is our model for patience: "But you, O Lord, are a God merciful and gracious, slow to anger, and abounding in steadfast love and faithfulness" (Psalm 86:15). Despite adversity, we can be gracious, merciful, and kind. In Hebrew, anger is literally tied with our physiology. The Hebrew word for anger also means nostril (אַפִּים). If you can think of a time when you or someone else was angry, you might also remember nostrils flaring.

An inherent part of patience is being able to surrender in the face of uncertainty. It is not a letting go, but the strength to endure until our hopes are met. As much as we may want something, there is always going to be some element that is out of our control. It is by faith and with perseverance that we keep our eyes on the prize. It is our trust in God and our response to act in the face of that waiting that brings us closer and closer to reaching our destination. Job is an excellent biblical example. Despite persistent and intense hardships, he was ultimately able to keep his eyes on God's sovereignty. Often, situations look dismal or uncertain. It is our hope and faith in God that pulls us through. It is God's grace.

God is patient with us just as we are to be patient with others. Patience is forgiveness in action. Each one of us is a work in progress. Despite our personal setbacks and failures, God works in our hearts, drawing us closer to love and goodness. We are not condemned by God but encouraged to be a fuller human being. Condemning others is not helpful. We can be patient with them. When we pray to God to forgive us our trespasses just as we forgive others who trespass against us, we are reminding ourselves to be patient and not condemn others. We are reminding ourselves to keep working toward our common good without falling into the cycle of revenge.

The Neuroscience of Desperation

In our patience, we wait and hope in the Lord. Without our eyes and heart fixed on our Lord, hope is easily lost. Being hopeless often involves losing confidence, the belief in the fulfillment of expectation, or the loss of trust. The Latin root of desperation means to be without hope.[42]

Desperation is usually characterized by sadness or despair. It can be accompanied by feelings of anguish, pain, and agony. The sense of hopelessness can lead to a wild, reckless pessimism that can move toward wrath and anger. Desperation can be both extremes of the flight or fight response. Hopeless desperation can also cause us to freeze and collapse.

Mentioned earlier was the calming role of the ventral branch of the vagus nerve. Especially in the event of trauma, the other branch of the vagus nerve, the dorsal branch, gets activated. When an event either is or seems so threatening that we become overwhelmed, it can cause the body to freeze and go into collapse. The body becomes flaccid, heart rate slows, breathing is shallow, and we become disassociated from our executive function. It is a state that can mimic death. These two branches of the vagus nerve create what is known as the polyvagal theory, developed by Steven Porges. The ventral branch (at the front of the body) is activated when we are calm. The dorsal branch (at the back of the body) is activated when we are so overwhelmed that the body freezes and collapses.

Desperation has negative effects not only for us but for our children. According to a 2018 review by psychologist Maria Gartstein and biochemist Michael Skinner, "When pregnant women feel more stress and adversity (as well as increased exposure to toxic elements like endocrine disruptors, alcohol, and tobacco), their children have a higher risk of depression, anxiety and negative emotions related to aggression."[43] This phenomenon is known as epigenetics. Genes can literally be turned on or off in utero as the baby develops. Trauma can be passed on from one generation to the next even before birth.

Another area that prevents us from the hopeful expectation of our desires is constant busyness. Busyness is of enormous opposition to patience. Our world is extremely hasty. We are invited to more, more, more in an ever-louder drumbeat. The mantra that is screamed at us is that bigger and faster are better, but in this state, we are constantly running on adrenaline. This is the stress response. Our body is made ready for fight or flight. When we are constantly busy, we do not give our bodies the proper time to rest and recuperate. We need to rest and recuperate. Being amped up and loaded with cortisol is truly killing many of us.

Irritability also leads to desperation. Being annoyed or agitated are generally states where the prefrontal cortex loses to emotional threat and an unhindered limbic system. Rather than focusing on a larger or more helpful outcome, the passion of the moment can take control. It can be a vicious cycle. Remembering to turn down our stress response helps the prefrontal cortex and executive function regain control. Irritability, annoyance, and impetuousness can also turn to hatred. Impetuousness often implies hostility or hatred. Hatred dampens our brain's circuitry that allows for tolerance. It also ramps up the motor circuitry of the brain as if to respond in swift action of retaliation. The hatred and wrath of desperation can also turn inward, including a sense of shame that manifests as real pain in the body.

According to the National Center for Posttraumatic Stress Disorder, in our country about half of men and women face traumas.[44] Many adverse childhood experiences can also cripple people into adulthood. In addition to personal trauma, there is much societal injustice. People are born into hardship and adversity. People are born into poverty. People are born into the cycle of trauma and often traumatize themselves and others without even knowing the full extent of it.

Without help from many others, we can be tossed on the waves of the ocean, where stressors keep us from utilizing our prefrontal cortex. Without turning toward love, we can practice hatred and revenge. If we do not practice the way of love, then the cycle of revenge will never stop. Sometimes not knowing why the world is as broken as it is can be difficult. It can cause us to freeze and collapse. Sometimes our expectations of God's goodness do not match with the reality of what we see in the world. This can be challenging, but ultimately, we can trust that our help and our strength is in God. It is God's will for us to respond patiently and with love. We can be part of the change in the world. This is God's will for us. If God is with us, who can be against us? If we rely on the precariousness of the world, we do not keep ourselves open to God's steadfast assurance. The world and the many things in our lives often seem against us. If our minds are attuned to solely looking for reassurance from the world about us, we will be sorely disappointed.

Brené Brown, in her book *Rising Strong*, speaks to how, when we are missing data points, we often fill them in with belief and fear to create a story in our minds. A story based on fear and false belief is a conspiracy. Many of us operate within our own conspiracies. These can be against ourselves or against others. These are partly what lead us into desperation. When we lose hope, it robs us of our joy. When we lose hope, we often work to rob others of their joy. There is always room for some sense of hope, no matter how dismal the situation.

Strengthening the Habit of Patience

In his book *The Fruitful Life*, Jerry Bridges details some essential aspects of patience. They include:

- Suffering mistreatment: Rather than retaliating or giving up, we can be steadfast.

- Responding to provocation: We can respond with love rather than revenge.
- Tolerating shortcomings: We can forgive ourselves and others rather than seek perfection.
- Waiting on God: When our expectations do not meet with reality, we can maintain hope.
- Persevering through adversity: Through endurance, we can gain perseverance and character.[45]

Being Steadfast Toward Our Goals

Patience without an end in mind is really just idleness. Without a goal, then patience has no meaning. Well-defined goals strengthen the executive function of your prefrontal cortex. Whether it's returning to good health, working toward something, or making some improvement, patience is always at work. If we are sabotaged in a goal, then we can exercise not wanting immediate revenge. If we face a setback, we can practice our patient perseverance. Being patient in our advance to a goal can also be witness to God. We can watch and wait patiently as the resources become available to achieve our goal. If success does not seem to come, we can patiently reassess our goal and how we are achieving it. An excellent way of practicing our patience is by having something to be patient for. Using the guidance below, set a goal for yourself and see how you work patiently to achieve it.

Here are several questions that can get to the heart of your hopes and desires for yourself. What do you love most about your life? How can you enhance it or relish it more? What do you dislike most about your life? How can you change it? What groups or people give you joy? How can you include them more in your life?[46]

Setting SMART Goals

SMART goals are goals set with purpose. They consist of five segments. They are specific, measurable, achievable, relevant, and time-bound. Use the table below to think of a goal for yourself to grow in one fruit of the Spirit.

Neuroscience and the FRUIT of the SPIRIT

Goal:

_____

_____

Specific: What actions will I take to achieve my goal?	
Measurable: What does progress look like?	
Achievable: Who will help me be accountable? How will I persevere in the face of challenge?	
Relevant: How can I make extra efforts not just feel like more work?	
Time-bound: What is the time frame I will accomplish the goal? How will I celebrate my victories?	

For Group Discussion or Personal Reflection

To go even deeper with our goals, desires, and motivations, we can begin with the end in mind and see our lives in the context of our death. This may seem morbid, but it can be extraordinarily life-giving and liberating to confront what we are most afraid of. Each of us will one day die. The petty grievances of today's world will all one day be very small when seen against the backdrop of eternity.

Take a moment to think about the following questions. What would I be most proud to have included in my obituary? How will I be remembered one hundred years from now? When I come before God at my death, will my life be a testimony of love?

_____

_____

_____

Palliative care nurse Bronnie Ware worked with dying patients for many years. She found that at the end of life, what people regretted more than their mistakes were the risks and opportunities they did not take.[47] Our deepest desires and hopes for our lives often get shelved because of busyness or habit, but we are alive today and can start toward God's dream of love and joy for our lives today.

Neuroscience and the FRUIT of the SPIRIT

Try this: Close your eyes and take a deep breath. Think of a time when you most felt enveloped in God's patience. If it is difficult to think of only one time, allow yourself to linger on whichever is the first example that came to mind. Do this for at least a minute, allowing yourself to relive the experience. Now with your eyes still closed, turn your attention to how your body feels. Perhaps you feel a sense of hope or purpose. Perhaps you feel awe and wonder. Where in your body do you feel these sensations? Describe below how it feels in your body to abide in God's patience.

_____

_____

_____

Keeping these sensations in mind, what one habit will you deepen to feel and relish God's patience working in and through your body?

_____

_____

Chapter 6 - Patience vs. Desperation

Try this with caution. Do not retraumatize yourself. If a memory comes to mind that is too challenging, use a different memory: Close your eyes and take a deep breath. Think of a time when you most felt desperation. If it is difficult to think of only one time, allow yourself to linger on the first example that came to mind. Allow yourself to briefly relive the experience. After fifteen seconds and with your eyes still closed, turn your attention to how your body feels. Perhaps you feel a sense of being lost, disoriented, angry, or afraid. Perhaps you feel like you're dizzy and spiraling down. Describe below how it feels in your body to be in desperation.

_____

_____

_____

Where in my life is there a sense of desperation? What Scripture, resources, or tools from this book will I use to overcome it?

_____

_____

_____

What habitual and settled tendency with my spouse, friends, family, or community is stuck in a cycle of hopelessness? What specific changes would create more systemic patience, steadfastness, and hope?

_____

_____

_____

What is one specific and measurable goal to create more patience and steadfastness that will help overcome a sense of hopelessness at an organization, church, or political group that I belong to? (Think with the end in mind: how will the lasting contributions of this organization, church, or political group be seen one hundred years from now?)

Goal:

_____

_____

_____

~ Pray ~

God, I am Yours. I say yes to patience, steadfastness, and hope.
I will challenge and overcome hopelessness and irritability.
I surrender to Your patience.

Chapter 6 - Patience vs. Desperation

chapter seven
Kindness vs. Hatred

A saint is a theatre where the qualities of God can be seen. ~ Rumi

Kindness (Greek – χρηστοτης – *pronounced krey-**stah**-teys*): The original Greek term for kindness also means integrity, excellence, or usefulness. In our day and age, we might also know it as altruism, goodness, or hospitality. It is about our connection to others.

The Habit and Theology of Kindness

Many of us are familiar with 1 Corinthians 13, Paul's beautiful ode to love: "Love is patient; love is kind; love is not envious or boastful or arrogant or rude. It does not insist on its own way; it is not irritable or resentful; it does not rejoice in wrongdoing, but rejoices in the truth" (1 Corinthians 13:4–6).

You may have heard this Scripture at a wedding. It might draw an image to mind of how we should treat others, but do we apply these words to ourselves? Apply this passage to yourself rather than simply to someone else: Am I kind to myself? Am I patient with myself? Am I rude to myself? Do I continually resent my mistakes? Do I ruminate over what I did wrong?

If we do not know how to accept, relish, and intend kindness toward ourselves, there will be no way to offer or intend kindness to others. Jesus's Great Commandment includes loving God, loving neighbor, and loving self. There are not just two parts to it, but three. Self-care is a biblical commandment. "You shall love your neighbor as yourself" (Mark 12:31). If we better understand how we connect to ourselves, it will help us better understand how we connect to others. This is the essence of the Golden Rule. Caregivers can also be taskmasters to themselves, not offering the same care to themselves as they do to those they help.

The theology of kindness extends to how we treat others. It is easy to love those who love us. God's challenge to us is to love those whom we hate: "Love your enemies and pray for those who persecute you" (Matthew 5:44). Despite our own failings, God loves us and invites us into deeper love. Despite the pain, loving our enemies is God's call to us. It is the only thing that can renew our world. Replacing hate with love is the essence of heaven. The deepest and most powerful kindness is being kind to those with whom we find it most difficult to be kind. It also reaps the greatest reward.

No matter if a person is a secular materialist, atheist, Buddhist, Jew, Muslim, or has no religious designation at all, we are called to love them. This also includes the hate-filled, broken, and even serial killers. Christ did not say to only love some of your enemies or just some of the people different from us. God is at work redeeming all who are broken even if it is exquisitely hard to see it. How we engage those who are broken or different from us says something about God's love at work in us. If we can love even those hardest to love, then our love will be a beacon of light.

Maybe if we can accept that which is best from those who are different from us, they will better accept what is best from us. Perhaps those who have declared that they have no religious affiliation might start thinking that there is something that we have that is appealing. The people we cut ourselves off from might start reconsidering when we say to them that some of their gifts are beautiful and amazing. They are not anathema. They are our partners in the way of love.

Neuroscience and the FRUIT of the SPIRIT

The Neuroscience of Kindness

Acts of kindness produce endorphins, neurotransmitters that help alleviate pain. Kindness can lower stress levels, which will decrease the effects of the stress hormone cortisol. Reduced stress will also help lower blood pressure. The social bonding aspect of kindness also helps produce oxytocin in the body. This is another feel-good neurotransmitter. With so many powerful effects of kindness, it is no wonder that we are hardwired to want to give and receive it as often as we can.

Studies have shown that giving and receiving kindness will increase the production of serotonin. Serotonin helps regulate our mood in the brain. Research shows that mirror neurons respond to kindness as if you are receiving kindness even as you are the one giving it. In other words, when a person gives kindness, their own mirror neurons simultaneously create an inner feeling as if they were receiving it themselves. This effect is known as the "helper's high."

Mirror neurons are stimulated when observing another person perform a task as if you are performing the task yourself. Neurons fire exactly as if making the movement yourself instead of merely observing it happen. Mirror neuron systems in the brain allow us to understand the actions and intentions of others. The better our minds understand how others act and intend, the better we can learn from them. Unless we develop our own capacity to understand and appreciate the actions of others, we will not have the empathy necessary to engage the world in love.

Mirror neurons come into play when we recognize facial expressions. You might be able to recall a time in your life when you saw someone get hurt and noticed that you cringed your shoulders as if you somehow felt the pain as well. In fact, basic emotional states expressed cross-culturally are incredibly similar. Anger, boredom, worry, joy, and fear can be identified in people in vastly different cultures simply by looking at their faces.

Imagine for a moment someone smiling at you. Do you feel joy? Perhaps it will make you smile as well. This is an example of mirror neurons at work. In this helper's high, our mirror neurons play a role in our feeling joy and love when we offer joy and love to others.

It is a natural euphoria because we are hardwired to feel the very love that we offer to others. This is especially the case when we see the cues and expressions of their joy and love of receiving our affection.

God's gift to us of mirror neurons allows us to understand and appreciate the fruit of the Spirit working in others because we are hardwired and feel the same fruit of the Spirit working in us. Love is hardwired into our being, and God has made it feel glorious to share it with others as it is being shared simultaneously in ourselves through our mirror neurons.

As you know them by their fruit, so too will the fruit of the Spirit be known in you vicariously. That we *can* know others are fruitful is a testament to the fact that we are hardwired to know and appreciate God's goodness. It is not only the goodness of others that we can recognize but also goodness working in us.

Perhaps this is why Jesus said that the Law and the Prophets hung on God's will expressed in the Great Commandment: "'You shall love the Lord your God with all your heart, with all your soul, and with all your mind.' This is the first and great commandment. And the second is like it: 'You shall love your neighbor as yourself'" (Matthew 22:37–39). The second is like it because it is based on love, for God is love. God's will is first and foremost about bringing our life and will into unity with love. We can focus our union with God through union with love. It is God's will that we live a fruitful life, and a fruitful life infused in the knowledge of our connection with God is an immeasurable gift.

The Neuroscience of Hatred

Hatred often causes people to want to fight. The neuroscience of the fight response involves many things. Rage will cause muscles to tense, breathing to become fast, and cortisol to be dumped into the system to create quick energy. Rage raises the heart rate. Pupils become dilated. Rage makes access to the frontal cortex more difficult. It is harder to think with our more executive reasoning. When enraged, we believe that threats must be contained, and this becomes our preoccupation. The amygdala plays a role in governing what is considered a threat and what is not considered a threat.

When our emotional response is disproportionate to the stimulus, this process is called an amygdala hijack. Just like a hammer might only see nails, if we allow ourselves to stop thinking with our prefrontal cortex and instead succumb to seeing the world as a threat, then we may opt to fight against it. Anger is often the result of fear. If we see that we are angry or have hatred, we might want to ask ourselves, what is it that we fear? If we see someone else with hatred, we might also ask what it is they are afraid of.

Through love, large parts of the cerebral cortex that govern judgment get deactivated. This is exactly the opposite of hate. Through hate, the brain works to calculate revenge and judgment. Numerous studies have shown that the neurology of hate "involves the premotor cortex, a zone that has been implicated in the preparation of motor planning and its execution." [48] Hatred mobilizes the motor system for defense or attack.

This is why the Lord's Prayer calls us to forgive others daily: "Forgive us our trespasses, as we forgive those who have trespassed against us." Hatred toward the other prevents us from loving them. We get locked into our own poison. Regardless of what the hated person is doing, the reality of our hate is within us. It prevents us from feeling love ourselves. That is why one of the most profound though challenging commandments of our Lord is to love our enemies (Matthew 5:44). Neurologically, hate actually harms us more than the person or object of hatred because we poison our bodies through a cascade of destructive neurochemicals. Stress hormones, high blood pressure, and intense ruminating are not good for us. Forgiveness is truly a gift not only to the one whom we hate but also to ourselves so that we can break the cycle of destructive neurological poison.

While the cycle of neurological poison within us is destructive, it also wreaks havoc on the physical world. Trauma and hatred are perpetuated from one generation to the next, often in an unconscious loop that devastates the most vulnerable among us. When children are faced with adverse childhood experiences due to neglect, abuse, and hatred, their lives are often stunted and cut short. Majority populations will often scapegoat minority populations, displacing fear through anger and tension. Cycles of hatred and revenge may seem somewhere out in society, but the reality is that these cycles live out and reside within our bodies. Different groups will possibly both hate and fear one another. They will isolate from one another. This trauma lives in us through the effects of chronic fear and anger and plays out in the world. Forgiveness of ourselves and others with acts of reconciliation are the only ways to break free from the cycles of revenge and hatred in our families, communities, and world.

Where hate directed at the outside world creates pain and self-loathing, shame directed inwardly produces pain, too. Shame is sometimes defined as anger turned inward. Anyone who has felt shame knows that it has a real effect of deep pain.

One of the deepest and most painful areas of shame for many Christians involves sexuality. Whether regarding pornography, masturbation, premarital sex, extramarital sex, abortion, LGBTQ+ identity, sexual abuse, or harassment, shame often prevents individuals from having healthy conversations that could lead to healing and better understanding even among disagreement. Dr. Lisa Sinclair, in her *Restoring the Paths: Sexuality for Christian Leaders*, provides excellent tools to help start conversations to move beyond shame. She reminds us that "too often we leaders are silent when our culture and media and peers are quite loud with alternative ways of educating."[49] Unless we face our own shame and have difficult discussions in the light of God's mercy, there is no room for healing.

"Be merciful, just as your Father is merciful. Do not judge, and you will not be judged; do not condemn, and you will not be condemned. Forgive, and you will be forgiven" (Luke 6:36–37).

Reflections to Strengthen Kindness

Kindness is tangible. Below are real actions that build up God's kingdom:

THE CORPORAL WORKS OF MERCY

Jesus listed some very specific actions we can take to offer mercy and kindness to others. He told us,

Neuroscience and the FRUIT of the SPIRIT

> Come, you that are blessed by my Father, inherit the kingdom prepared for you from the foundation of the world; for I was hungry and you gave me food, I was thirsty and you gave me something to drink, I was a stranger and you welcomed me, I was naked and you gave me clothing, I was sick and you took care of me, I was in prison and you visited me.
>
> (Matthew 25:34–36)

Through these corporal works of mercy, we are also drawn into awareness that our kindness is directed to Christ-in-the-flesh. When we offer kindness to others while seeing Christ in them, then our neural circuits are strengthened toward integrating our self as part of all things. Rather than simple actions, when our kindness is done in knowing that we are serving the living God, then all that we do is an expression of prayer. In offering kindness, God blesses us with feelings of euphoria through our mirror neurons.

FORCES FOR GOOD

To ask why someone is hungry in the first place is more powerful than only giving food to the hungry. Keeping people from sickness is more powerful than visiting them when they become sick. Unless we can change the underlying systemic problems of the world, then we are only addressing the symptoms and not the root causes. Leslie Crutchfield and Heather McLeod Grant in their book *Forces for Good* detail six of the best practices of some of the largest and most successful nonprofits such as Habitat for Humanity.[50] We might think of ourselves as small, but each of us is infinitely powerful. Remember the Butterfly Effect. If we can help the organizations we belong to follow these same habits, then we can change the world.

Advocate and Serve: To have high impact, organizations need to work with the government to make systemic change in addition to their acts of service.

Make Markets Work: Organizations need to embrace that the private sector and business models are not enemies. Having wealth is not a bad thing if we use our resources to help build the kingdom of God.

Inspire Evangelists: Meaning, emotional experience, and shared core beliefs will help inspire the organization to draw more and more people into its mission.

Nurture Networks: Collaborating with others is necessary. We cannot see others doing similar work as a threat, but instead, we need to see them as allies in a larger mission.

Master Adaptation: As science, culture, and systems change, we can adapt with them in learning, listening, and responding.

Share Leadership: The more opportunities there are to raise up individuals, the stronger the organization.

These ideas apply extremely well to a church. No matter what nonprofit, organization, system, or group we belong to, these six practices will make them stronger. Take some time to think about how your church or the groups you are involved with are using these six practices or could use them better. Which areas could you engage your church or organization more powerfully? Take some time to reflect on your ideas below and with whom you could share them.

_____

_____

_____

LOVE YOUR ENEMIES

> But I say to you, Love your enemies and pray for those who persecute you, so that you may be children of your Father in heaven; for he makes his sun rise on the evil and on the good, and sends rain on the righteous and on the unrighteous. For if you love those who love you, what reward do you have? Do not even the tax collectors do the same? And if you greet only your brothers and sisters, what more are you doing than others? Do not even the Gentiles do the same? Be perfect, therefore, as your heavenly Father is perfect.
> (Matthew 5:44–48)

Neuroscience and the FRUIT of the SPIRIT

If we all asked this question of ourselves every day and took it seriously, we could change the world in a heartbeat: Who is someone that I consider an enemy, and in what way will I love this person today?

_____

_____

_____

For Group Discussion or Personal Reflection

Try this: Close your eyes and take a deep breath. Think of a time when you most felt God's kindness working through you. If it is difficult to think of only one time, allow yourself to linger on the first example that came to mind. Do this for at least a minute, allowing yourself to relive the experience. Now with your eyes still closed, turn your attention to how your body feels. Perhaps you feel a sense of joy, gratitude, accomplishment, and connection? Where in your body do you feel these sensations? Describe below how it feels in your body to let God's kindness work through you.

_____

_____

_____

Keeping the sensations in mind from the previous exercise, what one habit will you deepen to feel and relish God's kindness working in and through your body?

_____

_____

_____

Try this with caution. Do not retraumatize yourself. If a memory comes to mind that is too challenging, use a different memory: Close your eyes and take a deep breath. Think of a time when you felt hatred. If it is difficult to think of only one time, allow yourself to linger on the first example that came to mind. Allow yourself to briefly relive the experience. After fifteen seconds and with your eyes still closed, turn your attention to how your body feels. Perhaps you feel a sense of tensed muscles, jaw clenched, heat, a furrowed brow, nostrils flaring, agitation, and anger. Is your heart racing? Describe below how it feels in your body to suffer from hatred.

_____

_____

What is one source of my hatred? What Scripture, resources, or tools from this book can I use to overcome it?

_____

_____

_____

What one habit or settled tendency is stuck in a cycle of hatred with my spouse, friends, family, or community? What specific changes would create more systemic kindness?

_____

_____

_____

What is one specific and measurable goal to create more of God's kindness to help overcome an ingrained practice of hatred at my organization, church, or political group that I belong to?

Goal:

_____

_____

_____

~ Pray ~

God, I am Yours. I say yes to kindness.
I will challenge and overcome my hatred.
I surrender to Your kindness.

chapter eight
Goodness vs. Ignorance

> Do all the good you can, by all the means you can, in all the ways you can, in all the places you can, at all the times you can, to all the people you can, as long as ever you can. ~ John Wesley

> But the hour is coming, and is now here, when the true worshipers will worship the Father in spirit and truth, for the Father seeks such as these to worship him. ~ John 4:23

Goodness (Greek – αγαθωσυνη – *pronounced ah-**gah**-thow-soo-ney*): uprightness of heart and life. Goodness can also be defined by virtue, excellence, or honor. Virtue is linked to a life principled by a moral sense of what is right and wrong. Goodness is also linked to strength, vigor, and generosity. It has an active quality.

The Habit of Goodness

Living a life of truth is one of the most basic and fundamental aspects of goodness. Beth Moore's study book on the fruit of the Spirit, *Living Beyond Yourself*, emphasizes how the quality of goodness involves zeal for the truth that is active and correcting. While a discussion on goodness could take many different directions, the primary focus here will be on one—a zeal for the truth. Unless we can confront falsehood and ignorance, we will continue contributing to the brokenness of the world. Living a life of truth starts with confessing our ignorance and acknowledging that each one of us has unconscious bias. Once we accept our limitations, then we can move beyond them. Strength lies in accepting our weakness. This is an active movement. To hide from weakness or put on a front of anger comes from fear.

The Johari window is a tool developed by two psychologists in the 1950s to help us acknowledge our ignorance. It plots out in four segments what we know and what is left unknown. It is a window into our unconscious.

JOHARI WINDOW

	Known to Self	**Unknown to Self**
Known to Others	**Open:** Public knowledge, things about ourselves known by others, and that we are aware of, too.	**Blind:** Feedback from others is needed for change.
Unknown to Others	**Hidden:** Private knowledge that can be shared if others are trusted.	**Unconscious:** Unknown to self and others. New awareness can be found. This is by far the largest of the four segments.

There is information that others know about us that we might not know ourselves. These are our blind spots. These could include mannerisms, beliefs, or ways of speaking. People have inherent biases that they are often unaware of. Allowing others to teach us is an extremely important life skill. The more we think about how we are ignorant and what our blind spots are, the better our habit will be of overcoming them. Remember the words of Jesus: "First take the log out of your own eye, and then you will see clearly to take the speck out of your neighbor's eye" (Luke 6:42). Take some time to consider what the log in your eye is. A picture of a log is included in the illustration above to help gently bring the point home! Ask a trusted friend or family member to point out some blind spots for you that would help you grow as a person. If we can start the habit of challenging our own ignorance, it will inspire those around us to challenge their own ignorance.

DEFENSE MECHANISMS

When it comes to moving beyond ignorance, examining how each of us uses psychological defense mechanisms is extremely helpful. People use both healthy and unhealthy mechanisms to help them adapt and cope. We are often unconscious of the defense mechanisms we use.

Unhealthy defense mechanisms include denial, delusion, or distortion. Rather than facing reality, sometimes people will create fanciful delusions to buffer themselves from the harsh realities of the world. Denying the truth outright and hiding within one's own cocoon is another way people cope. While about one billion people face food shortages throughout the world, in the United States, about one-third to one-fourth of food is thrown away.[51] To be unfeeling or uncaring toward the suffering of others is a way of living in a distorted reality. Perhaps feeling the weight of suffering seems too much for people to comprehend, so it is easier to put food in the trash than think of others who may need it.

One of the most tragic delusions of our time is our country's runaway debt of over twenty-six trillion dollars.[52] The interest payments thrown away each year on the national debt come out to about one thousand dollars per person. Imagine if each person in your household was given an extra one thousand dollars per year. For a family of four, that would be four thousand dollars per year! But we are throwing it away on interest, and the debt only keeps

Chapter 8 - Goodness vs. Ignorance

getting higher. Is it not delusional to be shackling our grandchildren's future into debt?

Other unhealthy defense mechanisms include acting out, projection, or passive-aggressive behavior. Perhaps anger is unconscious because one feels powerless in the world, and acts out in anger at their family. Perhaps someone is feeling vulnerable or afraid in their own situation, so they project and demonize others. Having a scapegoat might seem helpful in the moment rather than accepting the reality of being scared by one's own situation.

Not all defense mechanisms are destructive, though. Altruism, humor, and sublimation are healthy ways of engaging the suffering of the world. Rather than hide from the truth, an altruistic heart will propel us into action despite overwhelming odds. When we confront our own ignorance and prejudice, but can laugh at ourselves rather than punish ourselves, it will help us move beyond our limitations. Sublimation is one of the most profound of the healthy defense mechanisms. Sublimation is turning our tragedies into opportunity and strength. Perhaps someone was molested or raped in their youth. Rather than turning to anger and hurting others, they turn their anger into a life of advocacy for other people who have been molested or raped.

Living by God's goodness involves challenging our ignorance and unconscious bias. Where do you see yourself living by denial, delusion, distortion, acting out, projection, or passive-aggressive behavior? How can you break free from it?

_____

_____

_____

Healthy mechanisms drive us toward creativity and the birth of goodness through our hearts, minds, and actions. As discussed earlier, the Butterfly Effect demonstrates that each of us, no matter how small, has an infinite impact on our world. When we are geared toward creative goodness, we will change the world more profoundly than we can possibly imagine. Even the simple act of opening a door for someone or stopping to talk to a stranger will redirect every action and reaction they have moving forward in time and space. Every moment opens up infinite streams of connection into new realities for each of us. It has been said that our greatest fear is not that we are inadequate but that we are powerful beyond belief. We are powerful beyond all belief.

The Neuroscience of Goodness

If we can actively seek and engage the truth, then our neural circuitry will better mesh with the world. When we live in ignorance, we might be consciously or unconsciously drawn to ignore or dispute truth. If in our ignorance we feel cozy, then we will live in a cocoon. Neurologically we will have to make ever-larger distortions or delusions to separate us from the truth, or our fantasy world will get cracked by reality.

The hippocampus plays a major role in memory, but it is also essential in contextualization. People who often lie will have to keep track of whom they have lied to, about what their lies were, and the actual truth. This will put added stress on the hippocampus and neural circuitry just trying to keep track of the lies. A life lived in and by the truth will establish deeper connectivity with the prefrontal cortex and will give our brains deeper contextualization. The ventromedial prefrontal cortex (VMPFC), which is involved in moral and ethical decision-making, will play a substantial role in this. To engage and actively seek the truth will strengthen the VMPFC. A life grounded in truth will give greater flexibility and ease in making connections with our prefrontal cortex and our hippocampus's role in making memory because our memories will be true rather than a falsehood to deceive others. If we do not have to constantly think about our deceptions or the deceptions of others, then we can live in peace. We can live with less fear, anxiety, or suspicion of others.

Living life with less fear, anxiety, and suspicion is, in part, what makes a life of truth a life of goodness and generosity. The word *generous* comes from the same root as to give birth or be generative. Truth is the wellspring of goodness. It propels us toward trust and allows cooperation and collaboration. Without truth, suspicion and fear will rule our lives. Our conception of heaven is generally a place where truth reigns supreme. We can also work toward truth reigning supreme on earth as it is in heaven.

Seeing the world as it is can be overwhelming, but it can also fill us with gratitude. To know and be known is one of the most fundamental desires of all people. When we can see each other, "warts and all," rather than by deception, then there is much room for grace. In fact, gratitude and generosity work together. Gratitude propels us to give back and be generous. Gratitude and a generous spirit give us the ability to bring goodness into the world. Gratitude activates parts of the brain that produce feelings of reward, fairness, and morality. One area connected to gratitude is the medial prefrontal cortex.[53] The anterior cingulate is also involved because it is strengthened and activated when our thoughts and worldview are fixed on love and loving relationships. Seeing the world as it really is can be devastating, but if we live in ignorance and prejudice, our brains become convoluted by conflicting signals. Living in the truth helps us produce a cleaner conscience that is healthier and more capable of bringing about healing in the world.

Goodness also draws us to be creative and to work toward making the world a better place. When we are willing and able to see the world for what it is, then our prefrontal cortex can really get to work. The executive function of problem-solving can determine the challenges in front of us, and we can make plans and take action to overcome them. Continually looking to see the reality of the world will give us a clear conscience and help us plan for the best. The prefrontal cortex helps us understand long-term consequences rather than settle for short-term gratification.

The orbitofrontal cortex, in particular, helps us regulate pleasure-driven feelings. In his book *The Mindful Brain,* Dan Siegel details nine specific functions of the prefrontal cortex: body regulation, attuned communication, emotional balance, response flexibility, empathy, insight, fear modulation, intuition, and morality. The complexity and function of the prefrontal cortex are what set us apart from all of God's other creatures. Through the executive function of our brains, we can actively make plans to bring goodness into the world.

The Neuroscience of Ignorance

The thalamus plays a major role in our understanding of what is real or what is not real. If we believe something to be real, the thalamus will help make the perception become our reality. In fact, the thalamus does not make a distinction between inner and outer realities. If we approach the world out of fear and anger, then we might be drawn to shape our perception of the world out of falsehood and ignorance. Throughout our lives, we also get duped into believing falsehoods. Racism, hate, and fear often become unconsciously ingrained from one generation to the next. The brain is structured to perceive and act on threats as if they are real, even if they are not real at all.

Two examples of pathological neurosis are denial and delusion. When confronted with fear and anger, those who do not want to embrace the truth (or are so deeply unconscious of an alternative) will fight against the world. They will try to impose their own delusions on others so as not to have to face the harsh facts. As an example, many news outlets often sensationalize the horrors of the world and aggravate peoples' differences rather than strive for reconciliation between people of opposing views.

Passivity is one of the most destructive things at the heart of ignorance. Unless each of us actively takes part in reconciliation, love, and justice, the world will remain broken. If we take the world for granted, we will never overcome the horrors and sadness of it. Taking the world as it is, not asking questions, or not having curiosity, will all leave us in the dark.

Each one of us lives within a conceptual model of our world. As much as we would like to think that each of us lives in reality, we are limited by our senses, education, and cultural perspectives. Rather than denying our ignorance, we can embrace the fact that we only have limited information about the world. When we are surprised by new information and insights, then we can rewrite our understanding. We can seek truth. Once untruth and societal myths get hardened in our minds, it is hard to make a change, but through neuroplasticity, we are capable of great change. We do not have to live in ignorance.

Strengthening the Habit of Goodness through Cognitive Behavioral Therapy

Cognitive behavioral therapy (CBT) helps us overcome ignorance and destructive defensive mechanisms. It helps us make an action plan for change and see things as they truly are. The ABCD method is one of the simplest and most straightforward ways of using CBT. It involves reviewing an *activating event*, our *beliefs*, the *consequences* of our beliefs, and ways we can *dispute* our negative habits and beliefs. With help through a counselor or a group, it is very effective, though it is an effective personal tool as well.

Take a moment to think of one of the thought patterns that you have. Write it below and reflect on what triggers your belief in this pattern. Think of ways that you can dispute this negative thinking. You can also use the below for daily journaling. It will draw you toward goodness and away from fear and ignorance. It may be challenging, but it will be worth it.

Activating Event: What is the initial cause, and what continues to trigger a negative thought pattern?

_____

_____

Beliefs: What is the source of the negative belief, and what are the negative thought patterns?

_____

_____

Consequence: What are the consequences of your current way of thinking?

_____

Disputing: How could you relabel, reframe, refocus, or revalue your deceptive brain messages? What is an action plan for change?

_____

_____

Cognitive Distortions

The ABCD method of cognitive behavioral therapy will help us cut to the heart of our negative beliefs and the errors in our thinking. A cognitive distortion is an untruth that our mind is convinced is true. They are lies that we tell ourselves either knowingly or unknowingly. Cognitive distortions can destroy your joy and relationships with others. They can also damage your connection with God or the ability to experience love.

TWO COMMON COGNITIVE DISTORTIONS: FORTUNE-TELLING AND MIND READING

Mind reading is the assumption that we know what other people are thinking.[54] Perhaps body language, previous history, or what someone else has said about someone lead you to believe wholeheartedly that you know what another person is thinking. Examples can be: She thinks I'm stupid; he's not interested; he's angry with me; she's out to get me. Unless we ask the other person or verify our assumptions, our beliefs about another person could lead to unnecessary misunderstanding or even drastic consequences.

Fortune-telling is the prediction of a negative outcome. It could be for you or for someone you know. Examples could be: He's not going to come back; I'm going to fail; she's going to beat me; I'll have no chance. Below are some other very common types of cognitive distortions.

COMMON COGNITIVE DISTORTIONS

All-or-Nothing Thinking	Blaming	Taking it Personally
Only seeing black or white, right or wrong, good or bad. Using superlatives like "always" or "never." Also known as "splitting."	Always blaming others rather than admitting your own personal fault.	Blaming yourself or seeing things only from your perspective.
Should or Must Thinking	**Emotional Reasoning**	**Catastrophizing**
Often are associated with guilt or shame. Can be toward self or others.	Discounting empirical evidence and relying solely on emotion.	Consistently assuming the worst.
Halo Effect	**Discounting the Positive**	**Jumping to Conclusions**
Convincing ourselves that something is good when it is truly bad.	Minimizing or being blind to the good of our lives.	Sticking to a rash judgment without seeing evidence.

All-or-nothing thinking, also known as splitting, is one of the most destructive cognitive distortions. It is a way that we make in-groups and out-groups. An in-group is a social group to which we feel like we belong. Out-groups are social groups that we feel that we do not belong. This can be for a political party, ethnic group, or even feeling popular versus an outcast. Categorically dividing the best from the worst is one way that we perpetuate hatred. To see the other as "bad" will prevent us from loving them. This is why Jesus calls us to love our enemies. We are all part of the oneness of

God, drawn together in infinite mutuality. Any of the above distortions will get us into trouble.

Are you looking to go deeper to overcome cognitive distortions? *You Are Not Your Brain* by Drs. Schwartz and Gladding will give you more resources to relabel, reframe, refocus, and revalue your thoughts and impulses to receive God's goodness coursing within you.

Overcoming Ignorance through Body Awareness

Cognitive behavioral therapy is an excellent tool to overcome ignorance and destructive thought patterns, but unless we have greater awareness of our bodies, we will still remain in the dark. At the end of each chapter within the group discussion and personal reflection sections of this book, you will find exercises to help you slow down and be present to how the fruit of the Spirit works in your body or to feel when it is not working. With greater knowledge of the bodily sensations working in us, we will have greater awareness of the riches working in us. We will also be able to help other people name and celebrate how the fruit of the Spirit is working in their bodies.

There are exercises in this book to help you investigate indifference, anxiety, desperation, and hate. You might wonder why it is helpful to examine how our negative thoughts and experiences make us feel. We are often unaware of our negative thoughts because of past trauma or habit. To slow down and safely observe our negative thoughts and bad habits will help us overcome them. It can also help us teach others to do likewise.

Chapter 8 - Goodness vs. Ignorance

For Group Discussion or Personal Reflection

Try this: Close your eyes and take a deep breath. Think of a time when you most felt God's goodness by living truthfully. If it is difficult to think of only one time, allow yourself to linger on the first example that came to mind. Do this for at least a minute, allowing yourself to relive the experience. Now with your eyes still closed, turn your attention to how your body feels. Perhaps you feel a sense of clarity, purpose, lightness, or inspiration? Where in your body do you feel these sensations? Describe below how it feels in your body to abide in God's goodness.

_____

_____

_____

Keeping these sensations in mind, what one habit will you deepen to feel and relish God's goodness working in and through your body?

_____

_____

_____

Try this with caution. Do not retraumatize yourself. If a memory comes to mind that is too challenging, use a different memory: Close your eyes and take a deep breath. Think of a time when you discovered that your ignorance was hurting someone. If it is difficult to think of only one time, allow yourself to linger on the first example that came to mind. Allow yourself to briefly relive the experience. After fifteen seconds and with your eyes still closed, turn your attention to how your body feels. Perhaps you feel a sense of sorrow, being lost, scared, or confused. Describe below how it feels in your body to suffer from ignorance.

_____

_____

_____

What is one source of my ignorance? What Scripture, resources, or tools from this book can I use to overcome it? Who can I ask to help me see my ignorance?

_____

_____

_____

What one habit or settled tendency is stuck in a cycle of ignorance with my spouse, friends, family, or community? What specific changes would create more systemic goodness and zeal for the truth?

_____

_____

_____

Chapter 8 - Goodness vs. Ignorance

What is one specific and measurable goal to create more goodness and truth to help overcome an ingrained practice of ignorance at my organization, church, or political group?

Goal:

_____

_____

_____

~ Pray ~

God, I am Yours. I say yes to Your goodness.
I will challenge and overcome my ignorance.
I surrender to Your goodness.

Chapter nine
Faith vs. Falsehood

> But this is the covenant that I will make with the house of Israel after those days, says the Lord: I will put my law within them, and I will write it on their hearts; and I will be their God, and they shall be my people. No longer shall they teach one another, or say to each other, "Know the Lord," for they shall all know me, from the least of them to the greatest, says the Lord; for I will forgive their iniquity, and remember their sin no more. ~ Jeremiah 31: 33-34

> This is my Son, the Beloved; with him I am well pleased; listen to him! ~ Matthew 17:5

Faith (Greek – πιστις – *pronounced **piss**-tiss*): Faith is more than simply being persuaded of a truth. It is conviction of the truth in such a way that our lives become an expression of that truth. Conviction of the truth involves the active quality of showing what we hold firm in our hearts. Our belief involves the struggle and progress of making our whole selves align with the truth. Wholehearted faith is union with God and a life committed to God's will by aligning our body, mind, and entire system toward the truth. In Hebrew, the term for *heart* (לֵבָב) also means mind. Our mind and heart are one, just as our body is a temple whose parts all work together as a single unit. Like the prophet Jeremiah proclaimed, the new covenant includes having God's law written on our hearts and mind. It is not simply an intellectual activity, but an active investment of the whole self toward making God's kingdom come by complete commitment to truth, justice, and love.

The Habit of Faith: Making Our Lives an Active Expression of the Lord's Prayer

To live by the truth will make changes within our bodies. To live by the truth will help us overcome addiction. It is the overcoming of bad habits and sin. To make our faith alive and real, it cannot simply be an intellectual operation. At its most basic level, faith is an exercise of love. Faith involves love of God, love of neighbor, and love of self. It is through love that faith is revolutionary and can make change in the world.

Verna Dozier wrote, "Every time we pray the Lord's Prayer, we are praying revolution" (Thy kingdom come, Thy will be done on earth as it is in heaven). This is a call for revolution in our own hearts as much as it is to overthrow systems of injustice in the world. Not a violent revolution, but a revolution of the heart in doing our part to turn the world toward the will of God. The Lord's Prayer is central to Christian faith because it is the prayer that Christ taught us to pray and that he modeled in his own life. It cannot simply be something that we petition to God. It is a petition to God, but it is also a petition of change. It is a conviction of our own life and heart to worship God in Spirit and truth. It means being convicted to building God's kingdom on earth as it is in heaven. It is an expression of our willingness to participate with God in changing the world. It is a call to forgive. It is a reminder of our gratitude for our daily bread. Our most intimate prayers will change our bodies intimately and deeply.

Prayer is central to our faith, but we cannot simply petition God that God's will be done on earth. We must and ought to petition that God intervene on earth. The Lord's Prayer is specifically Christ's response to the question of how we ought to pray. The Lord's Prayer is foremost a prayer of action for each and every one of our lives. It is a personal affirmation and call for how we are to make God's kingdom come with all that we have and all that we are. If we are to follow God's will, then our prayer life will also draw us into serving the God of love through a life infused with love. If we are unwilling to be loving, then it is hypocritical to pray for God to do what we are unwilling to do ourselves.

Later in this chapter, you will find the Daily Examen exercise. It is an excellent tool to help open up the power and meaning of the Lord's Prayer in your life. It is also an excellent way of making love the expression of our lives. It helps us listen to how God is at work in our bodies.

The Neuroscience of Faith

A conviction of the truth becomes internalized and a part of our person. Three important parts of our brain that establish a sense of conscience that drives us toward the truth are the orbitofrontal cortex (OFC), the ventromedial prefrontal cortex (VMPFC), and the dorsolateral prefrontal cortex (DLPFC). The orbitofrontal cortex (OFC) is associated with inhibiting inappropriate social behaviors. The ventromedial prefrontal cortex (VMPFC) is involved in moral and ethical decision-making and making meaning of life. The dorsolateral prefrontal cortex (DLPFC) is associated with reasoning, planning, and executive function.

Research has found that when the DLPFC is more active, the VMPFC is less active. Conversely, when the VMPFC is more active, the DLPFC is less active. This suggests that when we act on a clear conscience, our thinking is clearer.[55] As an example, the idea of setting aside time to pray the Lord's Prayer to better follow God's will in your life sounds like pretty simple planning. Imagine planning to pray the Lord's Prayer and then, immediately after, going to spew partisan hate at your neighbors who have a different political view than you. The brain's ethical decision-making part, the ventromedial prefrontal cortex (VMPFC), should be in real conflict with the dorsolateral prefrontal cortex (DLPFC), the planning part of the brain, when these two very different activities are combined.

Being drawn to the truth and having a clear conscience are only part of what it is to be faithful. Every chapter of this book and each fruit of the Spirit works in us, producing conviction of the truth.

The neurological hardwiring toward peace, patience, and joy are ways that we become convicted of the truth. Neurologically, we overcome bad hardwiring and enter into the riches of the fruit of the Spirit when our lives become an expression of faith. If by faith we say that we accept the light but choose to live in darkness, then we are not living truthfully. Truthful living is aligning our thoughts, actions, desire, and will toward love. Scripture is clear on this: "If we say that we have fellowship with him while we are walking in darkness, we lie and do not do what is true" (1 John 1:6). Neurologically, our bodies will let us know if we are living in darkness or by the light. All we have to do is pay attention to whether we walk in hate versus kindness, joy versus addiction, or patience versus desperation.

A Theology of Faith: Conviction of the Truth

> For God so loved the world that he gave his only Son, so that everyone who believes in him may not perish but may have eternal life. ~ John 3:16

One of the most beloved and well-known reminders of whose we are is John 3:16. Because this verse is printed on billboards, bumper stickers, and T-shirts and conveyed through countless devotionals, most people are familiar with John 3:16.

This verse is central to the Christian faith. It provides support, comfort, and hope. It speaks of God's love for us all. It reminds us of our salvation. It is utterly beautiful and likely very familiar. But I would like to introduce you to just one of the original Greek words from this Scripture that will show you how much richer and more powerful it is, especially for how we understand our faith. That word is εις.

When I learned of this one word's meaning within John 3:16, I was astonished. I was in a Greek seminary course parsing out Scripture. I remember the professor saying something about it, and it sounded so very strange to me. It also sounded intriguing. It opened my mind, and I hope that it opens your mind, too. To have Scripture that is so rich and meaningful, and then to find out that it is more beautiful than we thought is one example of what makes grace so amazing. Just when you think your mind cannot be more astounded, then God opens you up to even more riches.

Having our mind opened by something unexpected is a key feature of our consciousness. If you walk preoccupied into a garden, your conscious mind might not register the trees, birds, clouds, or many of the details present. In any given moment, the brain is receiving and processing an enormous number of messages. In John's gospel, Mary Magdalene goes to the tomb and is confused not to find Jesus (John 20:11–16). Her conscious thought led her to believe she was talking with the gardener when, in fact, she was talking to Jesus. It was only when Jesus called her by name that her consciousness came to light, and she recognized that she was talking to her Lord and Teacher, *Rabboni*!

When our expectation is violated, it sends a very strong message that awakens our conscious thought. It causes us to think whether the new message is a threat or an opportunity. When we see something new in the familiar, it can wake us up to even more riches. It can open our minds and transform us toward the greater glory of God.

To allow John 3:16 to open our minds with even more power and wonder, the Greek word εις, usually translated *in* ["... everyone who believes *in* him..."], needs its time in the spotlight. This word includes several different meanings that are all very important. It is a small word but provides incredible insight about the beauty of our belief. This Greek word εις is pronounced like the word ice in English.

The word εις is used hundreds of times throughout Scripture and is very common. What is extremely interesting is that it is not always translated as *in*. The word εις is also translated elsewhere in the Bible as for, on, into, to, and toward. It might sound strange to think John 3:16 also implies to believe *for* him, believe *on* him, to believe *into* him, to believe *to* him, and to believe *toward* him.

The word εις is translated as *for* in parts of the Bible. In Luke 3:3, John is preaching the baptism of repentance for the forgiveness of sin using the word εις as *for*. When we look at John 3:16, we might also see how we believe not simply *in* Christ, but we believe *for* Christ. Belief is for God's purpose, but it also implies that by God's purpose we believe. By God's grace, we are drawn into belief and our faith compels us to bear fruit that will last.

Εἰς is also translated as *into* in many parts of the Bible. This includes examples of "into the house" or "into the land of Israel." In this sense, εἰς is used as lead us not *into* temptation or to be thrown *into* the fire. It implies moving from one place or condition to another. When εἰς is used in John 3:16, it implies moving from one place or condition to another. Our faith is mysterious and powerful. It changes us. We believe *into* God. This might sound utterly strange, but it captures more of what our faith is. Our faith is something more than mere intellectual consent. Faith is conviction, obedience, fealty, allegiance, fidelity, loyalty, and constancy.

Εἰς is also translated as *on*, such as in the example of seed falling *on* fertile ground. We believe "on him," implying that our belief stands *on* his grace and goodness working in us. Through faith *on* him, we allow the fruit of the Spirit to blossom through us. As Christ said, "For what was sown on good soil, this is the one who hears the word and understands it, who indeed bears fruit and yields, in one case a hundredfold, in another sixty, and in another thirty" (Matthew 13:23).

The word εἰς is translated as *toward*, as in Acts 20:21, by having "repentance toward God and faith toward our Lord Jesus." Elsewhere it is used as *toward* heaven. This implies that when εἰς is translated as "believe in him" in John 3:16, it also implies to believe *toward* him. Our faith draws us closer toward God. We are drawn into a deeper and fuller relationship with God.

Εἰς is translated as *to* on some occasions. This is most simply used in instances of a place, such as to Jerusalem or to Bethlehem, but it is also used as "to destruction." It might seem very strange to translate John 3:16 as "believe to him," but what εἰς implies is that through our faith, we come *to* a new state of being. Our belief draws us to be a new creation. We can be grounded in love, joy, and peace rather than any old conception of ourselves.

Like so many words that get translated from another language, we lose a part of what the original is conveying. To believe in God also implies to believe *to* God, to believe *into* God, or believe *toward* God. Any of these other ways of translating the word εἰς will probably sound very strange, but it matters because it sheds light on how belief is much more than a matter of intellectual assent. Our belief naturally draws us to bear fruit and live in relationship with God. Our belief will draw us deeper into knowledge and appreciation of our bodies, minds, and the reality of the world around us. Once we realize that our belief is about union, then our whole makeup can change. Sadly, if our minds are sure of our disconnect to something, it will appear real even if we are completely and absolutely connected. It's like telling a blind man that there is no water nearby when he is, in fact, sitting beside the edge of a lake.

If your understanding of faith is more integrated, then your prefrontal cortex will be more integrated with the whole system of your brain and body, and with the world and your larger reality. Our belief is about union. Union with God is union with love. We are reset, refocused, and repurposed. Emmanuel is the God who is with us. We are hardwired for love. It is the core of Christ's teaching. We just need to say yes and start reveling in it and sharing it with others.

We all have core beliefs, which are important to our sense of self and guide our decisions. I might believe that healthy eating is important. Someone else might believe that certain racial groups are inherently superior. Some people believe it is important to keep an open mind. Some believe in ghosts. *Dictionary.com* defines the verb phrase "believe in" as "to be persuaded of the truth" or "to have faith in the reliability, honesty, benevolence" of something. *Merriam-Webster* defines "believe in" as to have "faith or confidence in the existence of (something)." Going further, the *Online Etymology Dictionary*, etymonline.com, says, "Belief had by 16c [the sixteenth century] become limited to mental acceptance of something as true."[56] As Christians, our belief is more than mental acceptance. Our belief is all about union.

The *Strong's Exhaustive Bible Concordance* is a detailed study tool that identifies every Hebrew, Greek, and Aramaic word in the Bible and how it is used. Strong's definition of εις (#1519) is "A primary preposition; to or into (indicating the point reached or entered), of place, time, or (figuratively) purpose (result, etc.)"[57] Both of the prepositions *in* and *into* indicate relationship, but *into*, *to*, or *toward* further signify movement or change. These other meanings of the word εις represent movement from old to new, past to present and future, falsehood to truth, and despair to hope.

What we believe in is extremely important. We believe that God is all-powerful and all-knowing. We believe that God is love. Belief is essential but becomes most powerful when it is more than simply being cognitively persuaded of something. If our faith transforms us, then it is powerful. If, through our belief, we become a new creation and move into a new community and way of life in God, then it is powerful indeed.

Unless our faith integrates us with God's reality inside of us and God's kingdom throughout creation, we will not be in connection with truth. Because God is love, we can be integrated and connected. Love is about integration and connection. Love is about union and communion. If our belief draws us into a life of living by the fruit of the Spirit, then we will be integrated into love.

I invite you to reread John 3:16, but this time remembering that "in" also means into, to, toward, and for: "For God so loved the world that he gave his only Son, so that everyone who believes *in* him may not perish but may have eternal life."

To "believe into him" might sound unfamiliar, even strange. To "believe to him" or "believe for him" might also sound unfamiliar. These are not phrases that we're used to, especially when we think of John 3:16, but these other meanings of the word εις capture the fact that faith in God births something truly different in us. What happens when we "believe in" is not simple mental acceptance but a mysterious, awesome, and wondrous metamorphosis.

In *The Expository Dictionary of Bible Words,* Richard Lawrence wrote that the linking of belief with εις by the early church was never done in secular Greek and expresses the innermost secret of our faith. The New Testament "portrays a person committing himself or herself totally to the person of Jesus Christ, for our faith is into Jesus."[58]

To get a better picture of how powerful and unique our belief is, let's take a closer look at how εις is used in Scripture. I've bolded where εις is used in the original text in the New Revised Standard Version translations to remind you that it is translated very differently elsewhere in the Bible and means into, to, toward, or for.

Neuroscience and the FRUIT of the SPIRIT

I hope it is as striking for you as it was for me to find how often this word appears in the New Testament.

In John's gospel, εις shows up often (e.g., John 7:38; 11:25; 12:44; 14:1). Notably, in John 6:29, Christ says about himself, "This is the work of God, that you believe in him whom he has sent." Later, he expounds: "Very truly, I tell you, the one who believes in me will also do the works that I do and, in fact, will do greater works than these, because I am going to the Father" (John 14:12).

Other apostles applied εις in their writings about faith in Jesus: "Through him you have come to trust in God, who raised him from the dead and gave him glory, so that your faith and hope are set on God" (1 Peter 1:21). "All the prophets testify about him that everyone who believes in him receives forgiveness of sins through his name" (Acts 10:43)—everyone who believes into, to, and for the purpose of him.

In Matthew's gospel, we see the spiritual impact of believing in Jesus. An indivisible union is created between believer and the Lord. Matthew 25:40 says, "Truly I tell you, just as you did it to one of the least of these who are members of my family, you did it to me." Christ does not separate his community from himself. They have changed and become part of him. They have believed *into* him, so what is done to them is done to Christ himself. When the apostle Paul had his conversion experience, Christ spoke to Paul, saying, "Why do you persecute me?" (Acts 9:4). Paul thought he was persecuting Jesus's followers, but Christ revealed that his union with his faithful community of believers was such that their suffering was also his suffering.

Because we are neurologically hardwired for love, we can only live in harmony with ourselves if we are living in harmony with others. The first epistle of John 2:9–10 is a good example of this: "Whoever says, 'I am in the light,' while hating a brother or sister, is still in the darkness. Whoever loves a brother or sister lives in the light, and in such a person there is no cause for stumbling."

Paul reiterated these concepts of union with Christ and love for one another in his many letters to fledgling churches around the known world at that time. Underscoring his union with Christ, he said, "It is no longer I who live, but it is Christ who lives in me" (Galatians 2:20). About the unity and love between those who believe into Jesus, he instructed, "There is no longer Jew or Greek, there is no longer slave or free, there is no longer male and female; for all of you are one in Christ Jesus" (Galatians 3:28).

In his letter to the Romans, Paul articulated these concepts by relating them to baptism, the visible act by which early Christians publicly submitted themselves to Jesus's authority and the Holy Spirit's indwelling. Paul wrote, "Do you not know that all of us who have been baptized into Christ Jesus were baptized into his death?" (Romans 6:3). (Interestingly, while the New Revised Standard translation of the Bible often translates εις as *in*, we see in the NRSV that εις is, in fact, translated as *into* in this particular passage.)

This Scripture illustrates our earlier conclusion that life in Christ involves both death and rebirth. In baptism, we die to our old self—with all its principalities and powers—and God rebirths us into a new creation—with Jesus as Sovereign. In his book *Paul*, theologian N. T. Wright clarifies this: "Those who are baptized into the Messiah form the single-family; they have come 'into the Messiah,' they have 'put on the Messiah,' they 'belong to the Messiah,' they are 'in the Messiah.'"[59]

Through baptism, we become part of the body of Christ. We believe into this reality by changing the way we think and act. Since Christ's personhood and mission were characterized by love, we believe in, into, and for the one body of Christ by matching our thoughts, actions, and will with Christ's love. "God is love, and those who abide in love abide in God, and God abides in them" (1 John 4:16).

Why is this so important? It's important because the kingdom of God is wired within us and we get to participate with Christ in extending that kingdom outward into the world. That kingdom reigns in love. The Daily Examen exercise that you will find later in this chapter is so important. It is one of the most effective tools to focus us on God's work through our lives and to commit our will and actions toward serving God. It gives us a time of reflection to consider how we help build God's kingdom. Being focused on the concrete and tangible expressions of our faith and love is essential to being a follower of Christ. Gustavo Gutierrez's *A Theology of Liberation* is an excellent resource that details the importance of the concrete actions that help build God's kingdom. It is another resource to help draw out the importance of our living an active faith. As Gutierrez and others recommend, our theology is most powerful when it helps us liberate ourselves and others for a life of abundant love. If our theology is not about love, then we will be disconnected from the very way that we are neurologically hardwired. We are called to be a part of the saving action in the world through what we do, as an extension of who we are. The very meaning of the name Jesus in Hebrew is "Yahweh is salvation."

Living by Faith as if We Are in Heaven

Our salvation gives us tremendous hope for our future. There may not be an exact knowledge of what will come after this life, but there is conviction that there will be a new life to come. I believe a real failure of some church leadership has been not investigating the idea of heaven. Seeing heaven simply as a place in the clouds with angels playing harps is rather old-fashioned. But what, then, is heaven? We will never know the fullness of heaven in this life, but we can get a glimpse of it through Scripture and our own experience of God.

Pope Benedict XVI once wrote, "The essence of 'heaven' is that it is where God's will is unswervingly done. Or, to put it in somewhat different terms, where God's will is done is heaven." I believe all of us would like to think that about heaven. We would like to think that those who go to heaven will do God's will, that it is a place where we can trust others will do God's will, and that we can rest in that trust. If we live lives that cause suffering and we are hateful to others, why would God allow us to go to heaven and cause suffering, hate, and hurt to others there?

If God allowed hate and hurt to defile heaven, it would no longer be heaven. It would be like hell. Hell is generally considered a place of torment, untruth, and suffering. So, you could say, where the will of God is not done is hell. Wherever the will of God is consistently not done becomes hell. When truth and justice are not practiced, people suffer. We become the cause of our own suffering if we do not live by love. God's kingdom suffers without love.

The Daily Examen and Lord's Prayer are so essential to our faith because they both invite us to ask and to live by reflection on how we are serving God's will from day to day: Thy kingdom come, Thy will be done. On earth, as it is in heaven. We are invited to help make this world as it is in heaven.

LIVING BY FAITH IN COMMUNITY

I have seen in my lifetime the erosion of faith in religious institutions. Some studies and polls by Pew and Barna have found that especially among young people, religion is a negative rather than a positive.[60] It is to be distrusted. How tragic and sad this is!

Faith provides hope and strength. Active faith invites others to participate and gives a good reason why to participate. If our faith is not relevant, then it will die. God's kingdom is among us just as God is among us. When our faith is active and real, then we will see it at work in our bodies and through our neurological systems.

There are many national studies that have found a decrease in those who attend church regularly.[61] Studies also show a dramatic increase in those who do not ascribe to any particular faith tradition. This group is often referred to as "nones."

Those who have "none" as a self-designation still have a unique and personal form of faith. It might very well be that they want "none of that." They want "none of that" when it comes to so many people who proclaim faith, but live lives of hypocrisy. They want "none of that" when it comes to the extreme divisiveness and hate that is perpetrated in the name of God. The list of "none of that" could go on and on.

It is critical that communities of faith remain relevant. It is critical that our actions, worship, and liturgy reflect love. We must stay relevant and truthful to the Good News of Christ.

Worshiping in community should be about helping us believe in, into, and for the purpose of God. The primary act of this is our baptism. In baptism, we die to our old self:

> Do you not know that all of us who have been baptized into Christ Jesus were baptized into his death? Therefore, we have been buried with him by baptism into death, so that, just as Christ was raised from the dead by the glory

of the Father, so we too might walk in newness of life. (Romans 6:3-4)

The Baptismal Covenant of my own tradition in the Episcopal Church calls us to seek and serve Christ in all persons, loving our neighbors as ourselves. It also calls us to strive for justice and peace among all people and respect the dignity of every human. Baptism is not simply believing *in* something but believing *into* someone new. It is easy for all the promise of baptism to make us forget about the price. This is not to discount the joy in new life or our faith in the life to come. There is a cost to discipleship. We are to love as Christ loved.

Also central to communal worship is the sermon, yet neuroscience reveals that the congregation will only remember a small percentage of what they have heard. In what is known as the forgetting curve, psychologists have demonstrated that the majority of what we learn is forgotten over time.[62] I confess that I have forgotten the majority of the sermons that I have preached. If preachers do not equip their toolboxes with at least a minimal amount of neuroscientific knowledge, they neglect the mechanics of how their congregation hears, processes information, and is drawn into making concrete actions. Using cues of touch, taste, and smell all increase brain activity, helping the congregation remember the message. Dr. Richard Cox's *Rewiring Your Preaching* is loaded with tools and resources to help both pastors and congregants get more from sermons. The brain is attuned to act on information that brings healing and is useful for imminent survival. Cox puts the need for strong and informed preaching in succinct terms:

> The neuroscience of human learning, patterns of memory, methods of information retention, attention spans and other factors relating to how parishioners listen, hear, think and remember are available in lay language to clergy and laypeople alike. Ministers who do not consider this knowledge may be less informed of their primary task than their parishioners are.[63]

Cox refers to the process where the brain internalizes and accepts information as "engramming." Unless the preacher authentically accepts and demonstrates the message for himself or herself, it is highly unlikely that anyone from the congregation is going to act on it or find life in it.

Preaching mixed with youth and adult formation will also help the congregation retain what they have learned so that they can live in and for God's purpose. Mission and ministry are essential to any church so that members can be involved and formed through discipleship. If a church does not give its members opportunities for mission, ministry, or formation, it is likely that sermons will be forgotten.

We are invited into new life when we communally celebrate the Eucharist. St. Augustine said this brilliantly in his Sermon 272: "If you, therefore, are Christ's body and members, it is your own mystery that is placed on the Lord's table! It is your own mystery that you are receiving! You are saying 'Amen' to what you are: your response is a personal signature, affirming your faith. When you hear 'The body of Christ,' you reply 'Amen.' Be a member of Christ's body, then, so that your 'Amen' may ring true!"

Within my own tradition of the Episcopal Church, again after communion, we are reminded of our commitment to live into the life that Christ has called us in our post-communion prayer:

> Eternal God, heavenly Father, you have graciously accepted us as living members of your Son our Savior Jesus Christ, and you have fed us with spiritual food in the Sacrament of his Body and Blood. Send us now into the world in peace and grant us strength and courage to love and serve you with gladness and singleness of heart; through Christ our Lord. Amen. (*Book of Common Prayer*, 365)

Let us live *into* the likeness of Christ by serving God's will together. There is no better way than in community. We don't have to go it alone. The Lord's Prayer reminds us that we serve *our* Father. We pray to give *us our* daily bread. Forgive *us our* trespasses. These are all expressions of community and togetherness. Our faith is not meant to be a singular endeavor cut off from the rest of the world.

Neuroscience and the FRUIT of the SPIRIT

There are others like us who can help us and whom we can help. Find a church home and it will change your life.

The Neuroscience of Falsehood and Unbelief

> For the wages of sin is death, but the free gift of God is eternal life in Christ Jesus our Lord. ~ Romans 6:23

While much could be said about different types of belief or nonbelief, I would like to focus on one point. That one point is about how our faith either draws us into believing into and for the purpose of God or not. Paul wrote, "The wages of sin is death." We have seen with neuroscience that the wages of sin are, in fact, death. The truth becomes internalized in us and through us. If we live in sin, then sin lives in us. If we bring sin into the world, then we invite others to live in sin. We invite them to believe into and for the purpose of sin and falsehood. In their book *How God Changes Your Brain*, Andrew Newberg and Mark Robert Waldman detail how the "thalamus makes no distinction between inner and outer realities, and thus any idea, if contemplated long enough, will take on a semblance of reality." [64] Our personal and societal myths of falsehood become more true to us than reality because our brains become conditioned to see unreality and then try to convince the world that it is true. Two examples of myths not based in reality that people try to impose on others are sexism and racism.

On a further point regarding falsehood, research at Harvard on functional magnetic resonance imaging (fMRI) found that those who act dishonestly show greater activation in the nucleus accumbens. This part of the basal forebrain plays a role in our reward system. Prolonged focus on reward versus honesty can cause these circuits to promote higher levels of greed and lying. Continued lying, when someone is not caught, will decrease the emotional threat that the amygdala will register. As the discomfort of lying diminishes, the internal mechanisms to put on the brakes will disintegrate.[65]

Another important point about falsehood is how Jesus was very upfront about the sin of keeping children from knowing the love of

God. He said to let the little children come to him (Matthew 19:14). As discussed earlier, the lack of love and secure attachment with parents to children can produce false projections of how God relates to us. Without love and healthy connection, children often grow to be adults, projecting the same disconnect onto God that their parents shared with them. An angry or abusive parent will often draw a child to believe in an angry and abusive God. An anxious or avoidant attachment might also draw an anxious or avoidant relationship with God. We are to love one another and to love God. We owe it to our children to teach them healthy and secure attachment so that they do not project a false reality about God onto their future. We can believe into and for the purpose of God by submitting our will to the will of God, for God is love.

A final point about falsehood and unbelief that we can invite both atheists and ourselves to consider is this: Our world is a very broken place. There is much suffering. With our knowledge of the immensity of space, both believers and atheists can agree that the very fact that we exist and have consciousness is something exquisitely extraordinary. We can agree and believe together in the awe and wonder of our existence. It is an enormous falsehood not to work together with people who are different from us. With this extraordinary truth in mind, how will we work together to bring love, joy, and kindness to the world and overcome trauma and suffering?

Strengthening the Habit of Conviction to the Truth

Developed by St. Ignatius of Loyola, the Daily Examen is a powerful technique for seeing God's presence at work in our lives. I believe the Examen exercise and the Lord's Prayer are the most important exercises in this book because of how they build and strengthen our intention and attention.

They draw our prayer life and connection to God into an active expression in the world and through our lives. They also integrate our neural circuitry to focus and strengthen our connection with God's work in and through our lives. The Examen can be done for about 15-20 minutes at the end of the day or in the morning from the previous day's events.

The Daily Examen reflection is a way of opening up the Lord's Prayer and making it part of our daily Rule of Life. The examination calls us to see God at work: to hallow God's name and to see God at work all around us. The examination calls us to live our lives by God's will, drawing to mind how we are following God's will or not following God's will: Thy will be done. The examination calls us to ask for God's forgiveness just as we forgive others: forgive us our trespasses as we forgive those who have trespassed against us. It calls us to remember God's glory and power working in us. If we commit ourselves to daily examination, then our lives will be transformed into something glorious and powerful because we seek and serve the God of love.

The Lord's Prayer is the most succinct teaching of how Jesus taught us how to pray. When we pray it and petition that God's will be done, it is not with shrugged shoulders as if saying to God, well, if that's what you want, I guess I'll give in to it. God is not remote. God is always with us. As theologian N.T. Wright calls it, the Lord's Prayer is a prayer of submission and commission. It is a risky prayer. It is a prayer of subversion and conversion.

I invite you to pray and reflect on the following as part of your daily prayer practice.

The Daily Examen

Surrender – Lord, I am Yours. I pray that my life is an expression of Your will. (Take several deep breaths and as much silence as you need to quiet your mind.)

Thankfulness – What gifts from God are there in my day for which I give thanks?

Review – What are one or two ways that God has worked through me today? (Linger on how God has worked through you today in love, joy, peace, patience, kindness, goodness, faith, gentleness, or self-control).

What are one or two ways that I have not allowed God to work through me today? (Where have I created indifference, craving, anxiousness, impetuousness, hate, ignorance, untruth, prejudice, or volatility?)

Forgiveness – Lord, I am thankful for the times that I loved generously today and am sorry for when I did not. I pray for ways to reconcile with those I may have hurt.

Grace – Holy Spirit, I pray for Your fruit to grow in me, my enemies, friends, and neighbors.

I pray for one or two specific ways to help me and others grow in Your love tomorrow. I thank You for the ways You have inspired me.

I complete my time of examination by intentionally praying the Lord's Prayer:

> Our Father, Who art in heaven,
>   hallowed be thy Name;
>   thy kingdom come,.
>   thy will be done,
>   on earth as it is in heaven.

Neuroscience and the FRUIT of the SPIRIT

> Give us this day our daily bread.
> And forgive us our trespasses,
>   as we forgive those
>   who trespass against us.
> And lead us not into temptation,
>   but deliver us from evil.
> For thine is the kingdom,
>   and the power, and the glory,
>   forever and ever. Amen. (*Book of Common Prayer*, 364)

You might want to pray the Lord's Prayer using my example below, which elaborates more deeply some of the meaning.

> Almighty, ever-living God Who is Love,
> Sacred is all that reveals Your love and majesty.
> May all my desires and actions fulfill Your will. May the will of all match Your will and bring Your kingdom both on earth and in heaven.
>
> Give us today our nourishment as we commit ourselves to a nourishing life.
>
> Untie us from all that binds us, as we untie others who are bound by any ailments, afflictions, or addictions. May we work toward our own liberation and the liberation of all.
>
> Help us not to enter into temptation but deliver us from evil. May we also contemplate how our lives might produce evil and stop any ways we contribute to it in our hearts, home, community, nation, and world.
>
> For all is Yours and ever will be Yours; May all that I do draw me and others deeper and deeper into Your splendor, Your wonder, and Your power, forever and ever. Amen.

The Daily Examen is the most important exercise in this book because it helps us examine how the fruit of the Spirit is working in us each day. It allows us to thank God for the gifts that we receive.

It allows us to celebrate those gifts over time as they become stronger and more beautiful. It also allows us to acknowledge our sin and the bad fruit working in us. It attunes us to receive God's grace and envelopes our life in prayer. It provides us hope for the days to come.

Neuroscience and the FRUIT of the SPIRIT

For Group Discussion or Personal Reflection

Daily Examen: The root of the word *devotion* means putting down one's vow, fealty, or allegiance. By examining daily how we live out our faith by the fruit of the Spirit through love, joy, and patience, we can track how we are living or not living by God's will. If you make this part of your daily practice, it will eventually become a pivotal part of how you view the world so that every moment of your life is intentional in following God's will of love.

How can the Daily Examen strengthen your active expression of faith?

_____

_____

_____

How can the Daily Examen help you live by the Lord's Prayer?

_____

_____

_____

Try this: Close your eyes and take a deep breath. Think of a time when you most felt faithful to God. If it is difficult to think of only one time, allow yourself to linger on the first example that came to mind. Do this for at least a minute, allowing yourself to relive the experience. Now with your eyes still closed, turn your attention to how your body feels. Perhaps you feel a sense of confidence, direction, clarity, or embrace? Perhaps you feel God's presence?

Where in your body do you feel these sensations? Describe below how it feels in your body to be faithful to God.

_____

_____

_____

Keeping these sensations in mind, what one habit will you deepen to feel and relish God's faithfulness working in and through your body?

_____

_____

_____

Try this with caution. Do not retraumatize yourself. If a memory comes to mind that is too challenging, use a different memory. Close your eyes and take a deep breath. Think of a time when you lived in or by falsehood. If it is difficult to think of only one time, allow yourself to linger on the first example that came to mind. Allow yourself to briefly relive the experience. After fifteen seconds and with your eyes still closed, turn your attention to how your body feels. Perhaps you feel a sense of inner conflict, turmoil, headache, butterflies in the stomach, or fear of being exposed? Describe below how it feels in your body to live in falsehood.

_____

_____

_____

Neuroscience and the FRUIT of the SPIRIT

What do you look forward to doing in heaven?

_____

_____

_____

If your list did not include love, kindness, or service to God, why not? What Scripture, resources, or tools from this book can you use to help create heaven on earth?

_____

_____

_____

What one habit or settled tendency is stuck in a cycle of falsehood with my spouse, friends, family, or community? What specific changes would create more systemic conviction to the truth?

_____

_____

_____

Chapter 9 - Faith vs. Falsehood

What is one specific and measurable goal to create more faithfulness to help overcome an ingrained practice of falsehood at my organization, church, or political group?

Goal:

_____

_____

_____

~ Pray ~

God, I am Yours. I say yes to faithfulness.
I will challenge and overcome my falsehood and unbelief.
I surrender to Your faithfulness.

chapter 10
Gentleness vs. Prejudice

My grace is sufficient for you, for my power is made perfect in weakness. ~ 2 Corinthians 12:9

Whoever becomes humble like this child is the greatest in the kingdom of heaven. Whoever welcomes one such child in my name welcomes me. ~ Matthew 18:4–5

Gentleness (Greek – πραυτης – *pronounced prah-oo-teys*): Having the quality of humility. Freedom from arrogance or excessive pride. It also involves the ability to remain calm in the face of hostility. Other ways of viewing gentleness involve mildness or meekness. As Jesus said, "Blessed are the meek, for they will inherit the earth" (Matthew 5:5).

The Habit of Gentleness

While much can be said of gentleness, there are three habits that I think are extremely important. The first is listening. If we are able to listen, then we are able to be affected. When we allow ourselves to hear, we open up a dialogue that we may also be heard. To be heard is to be known. To be known and understood is perhaps one of the best gifts that we can give to others and to ourselves.

A second habit of gentleness is forgiveness. Scripture is clear that in forgiving others, our heavenly Father forgives us (Matthew 6:14). In forgiving, the hate and anger that we harbor can be released. This will have a profound effect on our health. In Aramaic, the language of Jesus, the term for forgiveness was *shabaq*. This meant to be unbound or untied. To loose the chains of hatred and desire for revenge loosens the bonds on our heart against others. It allows for healing and change—not just in reconciliation, but for our own good as well.

A third habit of gentleness is vulnerability. To be vulnerable is allowing ourselves to be wounded. In fact, the word vulnerable comes from a root word, which means wound. When we are courageous and expose our heart, sometimes it will be wounded. But unless we can be courageous, we will not be able to change the world. We will not be able to change ourselves. The word *courage* has significance. Courage comes from a root word that means heart. To have heart and to be wounded are two of the most fundamental aspects of being gentle.

The act of confession is so powerful partly because it draws together listening, being heard, vulnerability, forgiveness, and courage. We should not underestimate the healing that can come from confession. Whether through spiritual direction, in corporate worship, or in our private dialogue with God, confession of our sins will help us move beyond them.

The Neuroscience of Gentleness

Hiding from fear does not allow us to deal with it. It can even become more powerful as we are afraid to even address a weakness. It can make us even more anxious by trying to hide from our vulnerability. We can be fiercely alive by drawing it out and working through it.

If a group is willing to be vulnerable together, then they will have the strength of working through conflict. The hippocampus helps store and create memories. When someone feels comfortable with those around them, they will be invited to share the content of their memories. If the environment is hostile, or others do not draw out risky or vulnerable areas with one another safely, people may

Neuroscience and the FRUIT of the SPIRIT

unconsciously or consciously hide memories and details that might show weakness. Unless a group is able to investigate and overcome their weaknesses together in safety, those weaknesses will remain but in unspoken or hidden ways. Extreme fear will sometimes result in deep psychological defense mechanisms that are not based in reality. Deep fear might cause people to live in delusions or paranoia, but with courage, we can see what is true and real. We can engage our weak spots and allow others to see our own.

What might seem like a weakness, such as showing a vulnerability, is actually a strength as it allows weak spots to be addressed and overcome. Addressing perceived weaknesses together allows for creativity and adaptation. It allows for growth and change.

The Neuroscience of Prejudice

One might argue that hardness would be the opposite of gentleness. Neurologically, prejudice is just that. When our hearts have become hardened in positions that do not correlate to reality, then real hurt can occur. This is hurt not just to others but also to ourselves. When we move through the world in either conscious or unconscious bias, we do not allow ourselves to open up to possibilities. We can be wrecking balls of hate without even knowing it.

Prejudice is generally defined as a preconceived judgment or irrational attitude. It often involves hostility. Prejudice can be callous or harsh. It prevents the truth from being heard. It is the ground of discrimination and animosity.

There are several parts of the brain associated with prejudice. The amygdala involves our association with threats. As the mind creates and maintains understanding of threats, our ideas can become reinforced. The anterior insula involves the process of negative affect. The medial prefrontal cortex (MPFC) helps put things in perspective and bring them into a mental picture. While the MPFC helps us categorize the world, the downside is that our categorizations can be completely false though they seem real to us. All these structures taken together help categorize in-group and out-group.[66] Positive attitudes toward an in-group are supported by the striatum. Part of the striatum is the nucleus accumbens, which is part of the brain's reward center. The more we feel accepted by a social group, the more we feel rewarded.

Within cultural contexts, when we are told to believe stereotypes and prejudice, the neural circuitry to perpetuate hate gets strengthened and then passed on to the next generation. Sadly, prejudice can be either conscious or unconscious. Many people who are full of hate might not realize there is another way because of how they were raised or taught. Prejudice is a poison that lives in the body that oozes out into the world. Prejudice and hate often move from generation to generation in a cycle of trauma, and it is our children who become the victims of this horrible cycle.

Strengthening the Habit of Gentleness

> And the point is, to live everything. Live the questions now. Perhaps you will then gradually, without noticing it, live along some distant day into the answer. ~ Rainer Maria Rilke

The habit of gentleness involves being comfortable with questions. It involves being comfortable questioning ourselves but also questioning others with love and kindness. There is an enormous amount of freedom in giving ourselves permission that we have not figured it all out. Who of us has ever really figured it all out? Those trying to convince themselves that they have are probably the ones that have not. We are all in the process of knowing more about ourselves and knowing more about others. Getting comfortable with questioning ourselves and others involves being comfortable with listening.

The art of listening takes practice and skill. When we listen to others, we can lean forward, so that they know we are listening. We can avoid looking away or being distracted.

Dr. David Gortner's *Transforming Evangelism* describes how powerful it is to invite others to share their stories of transformation and encounters with God.[67] When we become more adept at listening to others, we also become more adept at hearing God's work in our own lives. The more we invite others to name, share, and celebrate God's work in their lives, the more comfortable we ourselves can become. We can walk as fellow pilgrims rather than act as if we have all the answers.

One of the most powerful listening skills is a well-placed, open-ended question. Rather than asking a yes or no question, we can ask open-ended questions to spark conversation. Open-ended questions generally start with "how," "why," or "what." If you ask a question with someone using how, why, or what, it is harder to reply with simply a yes or a no. Open-ended questions will allow you to hear and listen to the heart. An open-ended question also says that you are looking for a deeper opportunity to listen rather than a simple yes or no answer.

Open-ended questions are just one of many active listening skills. The listening skills below are extremely helpful in gently affirming and engaging the heart of others.

Active Listening and Intentional Question Skills

Literal Repetition: Feeling heard, understood, and known are very important. To repeat back what someone has said shows that you care and have been listening.

Reflecting: A way of rearticulating the emotional content of what is being said. Example: "It sounds like you've had a long and overwhelming day . . ."

Paraphrasing: Rewords dialogue for the speaker and lets them know that you have been listening. Example: "I hear you saying that . . ."

Summarizing: Can help focus on the emotional content of what is being said. Example: "It sounds as if you're feeling . . ."

Open-Ended Questions: Avoid a yes or no response. These questions will often begin with how, why, or what. They could also begin with did or does. Example: "What's on your mind tonight?" instead of "Is there something on your mind?"

Buffering: Can help soften a difficult emotion. As an example, "You may not want to talk about this now, but . . ."

Understatement / Euphemism: If something seems understated, it can be drawn out in case the speaker might be unconsciously hiding from it.

Tell Me More / Minimal Encouragement: Helps the speaker know that your interest and attention are with them. Example: "Tell me more about . . ."

Calling Attention: Pointing out something that may be unnoticed or unconscious such as tears. Example: "I saw some tears welling up in your eyes. What's on your heart?"

Hovering: If the topic is painful or risky, it can help bring the dialogue back on track if the speaker touches on something but then moves to another subject.[68]

Try This:
Host a small group dinner inviting friends and neighbors to share about their faith using open ended questions. The website www.sharingfaithdinners.com has many excellent questions and resources to reflect on God together. You might be surprised to learn deep insights about the faith of people you have known for years!

WATCHING FROM THE BALCONY

There is a group dynamic expression called watching from the balcony that is another excellent listening skill. The premise is that when we engage with others, we remain vigilant in monitoring our own thought process and assessment of what might be going on behind the conversation. It's something like intentionally listening to yourself listen or listening to the unspoken emotional content behind what is being vocally said. Watching from the balcony asks about what is not communicated directly. What are the hidden emotions, or what is left unsaid? How might we draw these things out to help in healing?

When we listen from the balcony, we can also listen to see how God might be at work. Where is there an opportunity for reconciliation? How is a person being heard so that they might find forgiveness? Being intentional and paying attention to the subtleties of our social reality will show us much at work.

LISTENING TO OTHERS WITH WHOM WE DISAGREE

The simple act of hearing another person can diffuse anger. Find the strongest point of another person's argument and give them credit for their sincerity. This can be reflected back to them so that they feel heard. Avoid classifying a person, but rather separate their argument from a broad generalization of who the person may seem to be. Never ridicule but remember that God is already at work in your conversation and ask yourself how God would hope you to proceed. When listening to someone you disagree with, pray for them. Pray for yourself to have the right words to respond in love. Give yourself permission to disagree with someone while still engaging them with love and kindness. Give the other person permission to disagree with you. If you disagree on one point, or even many points, find something that you do agree with. Work together to make a change in the world on that point or other points that are deeply important to both of you.

Chapter 10 - Gentleness vs. Prejudice

For Group Discussion or Personal Reflection

Try this: Close your eyes and take a deep breath. Think of a time when you allowed God's gentleness to work through you. If it is difficult to think of only one time, allow yourself to linger on the first example that came to mind. Do this for at least a minute, allowing yourself to relive the experience. Now with your eyes still closed, turn your attention to how your body feels. Perhaps you feel a sense of clarity, release, comfort, focus, or peace. Describe below how it feels in your body to offer God's gentleness.

_____

_____

_____

Keeping these sensations in mind, what one habit will you deepen to feel and relish God's gentleness working in and through your body?

_____

_____

_____

Try this with caution. Do not retraumatize yourself. If a memory comes to mind that is too challenging, use a different memory: Close your eyes and take a deep breath. Think of a time when you felt prejudice. This could be either prejudice toward you or your own prejudice toward another person or group. If it is difficult to think of only one time, allow yourself to linger on the first example that came to mind. Allow yourself to briefly relive the experience. After fifteen seconds and with your eyes still closed, turn your

Neuroscience and the FRUIT of the SPIRIT

attention to how your body feels. Perhaps you feel a sense of anger, disconnect, uncertainty, or fear. Perhaps you feel sad. Describe below how it feels in your body to suffer from your own prejudice or the prejudice of someone else.

_____

_____

_____

What is one source of my prejudice? What Scripture, resources, or tools from this book can I use to overcome it?

_____

_____

_____

What one habit or settled tendency is stuck in a cycle of prejudice with my spouse, friends, family, or community? What specific changes would create more systemic gentleness and listening by overcoming it?

_____

_____

_____

Chapter 10 - Gentleness vs. Prejudice

What is one specific and measurable goal to create more gentleness and listening to help overcome an ingrained practice of prejudice at my organization, church, or political group?

Goal:

_____

_____

_____

~ Pray ~

God, I am Yours. I say yes to gentleness.
I will challenge and overcome my prejudice.
I surrender to Your gentleness.

chapter eleven
Self-Control vs. Volatility

Everybody thinks of changing humanity and nobody thinks of changing himself. ~ Leo Tolstoy

All of our life, so far as it has definitive form, is but a mass of habits. ~ William James

Self-Control (Greek – εγκρατεια – *pronounced eg-**krah**-teh-ee-ah*): Is the mastery of our desires. What we desire, long for, expect, or demand can define our reality unless kept in check. Self-control is also historically associated with temperance, moderation, and self-restraint.

The Habit of Self-Control

The habit of self-control might be seen as organized, controlled, or regimented. The habit of being controlled or regimented does not generally bring a picture of joy to the mind.

Richard Foster's *A Celebration of Discipline* is an excellent book that helps dispel the myth that a disciplined life is without joy. In his book, Foster elaborates classical spiritual disciplines such as prayer, study, meditation, fasting, and simplicity and how our commitment to them brings us more life rather than less. Creating discipline in our life helps open doors. It helps bring freshness. Like crawling into a bed with fresh sheets, it can feel cozy and delightful. Where there is discipline, the door can be opened to wonder, awe, and an opportunity to be lost in the moment. If we are overwhelmed by all the things in our lives or feel disorganized, then there will be no room to see a larger perspective. Habits that build discipline and structure can be seen as joyful in themselves. The more proficient we become at habits that help us gain self-control, the easier and easier they will become until they become a part of us.

The Neuroscience of Self-Control

Neurons that fire together wire together. We have discussed this basic principle of neuroscience known as Hebb's Law. The more we do something, the stronger the habit becomes. Habit formation is partly ingrained in an area of the brain called the basal ganglia. The basal ganglia get strengthened as habits get more engrained so that habits become easier and more automatic. A major component of the basal ganglia is the nucleus accumbens. The nucleus accumbens releases dopamine, which is central in our reward system.

According to some neuroscientists, "about 80 percent of the neural instructions for behavior are recorded in implicit memory, outside our conscious awareness."[69] Neurologically, habits work in a loop that contains a cue, routine, and reward.[70] What makes up our habits is often outside of our conscious awareness. Isolating the cue, routine, and reward of a habit can help us see why we do the things we do. There is often a trigger that sends our minds into automatic mode. Imagine a commercial of an ice-cold beverage or a mouth-watering sandwich. Those are powerful cues that compel us to act.

Our routines can be emotional, physical, or psychological. It could be a thought pattern or something like going to the refrigerator late at night. The reward is something that your brain uses to remember this pattern even without thinking. Our memories are encoded with emotional content that will produce real feelings of euphoria or disgust. When you isolate the reward, it can help to change the routine. If the reward of your routine is to feel connection, perhaps spending time with family is a better routine than watching the news for hours per day.

The habit of regular exercise is one of the best in forming new neural pathways. It increases blood flow to the brain. Exercise improves cognition. It reduces anxiety. It boosts immune function. It can increase the level of the neurotransmitter GABA, which can suppress depression. Aside from physical exercise, if we exercise all the habits that form the fruit of the Spirit reviewed in this book, then we can gain self-control in our lives. We can remember that our bodies are temples of the Holy Spirit. Through God's help and prayer, we can be transformed.

We must be gentle with ourselves. Sometimes, no matter how much effort we exert, it is not enough. We can reach out for the help of others. If not friends and family, a trusted counselor can help us through whatever darkness we face. It is not helpful to judge ourselves or others if we cannot succeed. Sometimes the help of antidepressants or antianxiety medication can make all the difference. Our brains are organs like any other. Sometimes they need medicine to help them function better. Each of us has organs that will not function perfectly at some point in our lives. We can be gentle with ourselves and others, knowing that medication might be our very best option to help make the progress we need.

The Neuroscience of Volatility

Volatility is generally a tendency for quick or unpredictable change for the worse.

Lack of sleep leads to agitation. Not having proper nutrition leads to an inability to think. If the habit of our mind is to ruminate on past mistakes or future anxiety, then we will be like a wave tossed on the ocean. If we allow fear or aggression to consume us, then these habits will have power over us. They will possess us. If we do not resist our fear and anger, the amygdala might get structured to wire our brains to perceive constant threat and compel us to fight. Prolonged fear and anxiety will damage structures like the hippocampus and anterior cingulate that help stop the stress response and draw us toward love.

Stress, along with a bad diet and inactivity, can lead to prediabetes. According to the Centers for Disease Control and Prevention, approximately eighty-four million American adults have prediabetes. "Insulin is a hormone made by your pancreas that acts like a key to let blood sugar into cells for use as energy. If you have prediabetes, the cells in your body don't respond normally to insulin. Your pancreas makes more insulin to try to get cells to respond."[71] Over time your body just can't keep up. Through stress, inactivity, and poor diet, we can develop prediabetes. Prediabetes leads to type 2 diabetes. Diabetes can be life-threatening and debilitating.

Through healthy boundaries, we can stay healthy. Through prayer and meditation, we can change our default mode network. We do not have to be governed by fear and anxiety. Our body and mind can be strengthened. Living by God's laws helps break us free from the volatility in the world. Societal sins and prejudices, which are prevalent in the current news cycle, do not have to be how we view the world.

Strengthening the Habit of Self-Control

Habit, if not resisted, soon becomes necessity. ~ Saint Augustine

Three essential ways of mastering our bodies and minds are through proper nutrition, sleep, and exercise.

NUTRITION AND HYDRATION

The National Academies of Sciences, Engineering, and Medicine determined that adequate daily fluid intake is about 15.5 cups for men or about 11.5 cups a day for women.[72] This covers fluid from water, beverages, or food. About 20 percent of fluids will come from foods. An easier metric that is commonly cited is to drink eight 8-ounce glasses of water a day. Dehydration is one of the most common causes of headaches. The simple habit of hydrating can mean a world of difference in your life.

When it comes to nutrition, eating well is not simply about healthy balanced meals. It is also about having the right relationship with food. In her poem "Rice," Mary Oliver brings the food to life: "I don't want you just to sit down at the table. | I don't want you just to eat and be content. | I want you to walk out into the fields, | where the water is shining and the rice has risen."[73] In every bite of food, there are thousands of hours of nourishment. From the hours it takes to plant, harvest, transport, prepare, package, and deliver food to the local market, there is love and care in our food. To eat a salad might put together produce from several different countries. How did the sun kiss each vegetable over time? What rains and winds swept over the kernels of corn? We can enter into the blessing of our nourishment by appreciating how intricately beautiful and complex it is.

Are you eating when you feel hungry or eating because of unhealthy cravings? The hormone leptin helps decrease your appetite. It is produced by fat cells. Becoming obese can be the result of building up a resistance to leptin. If we are not intentional about our eating, then it can become unhealthy and based on mindless cravings. The hormone ghrelin helps increase appetite, and you can feel it when you're hungry.[74] If we habitually build up resistance to what our body is naturally telling us, it can be tragic.

The gut-brain connection is one of the most exciting areas of science and extremely important in our nutrition. Earlier in this book, it was mentioned that you are an ecosystem. You have roughly one hundred trillion bacteria living in your gut. It is like commanding a vast army that is either for or against you. Excessively fatty foods produce unhealthy bacteria that can also lead to further cravings. Highly refined and sugary foods also have a negative effect on your gut bacteria. Microbes that yield positive effects, called psychobiotics, help with digestion, your immune response, and even your mood. Psychobiotic bacteria such as Lactobacillus (Lacto) and Bifidobacterium (Bifido), especially found in yogurt, are healthy for us. Bifido produces butyrate, which can "induce a good mood, dampen inflammation, or encourage the production of brain-growth hormone."[75] Bifido thrives on the fiber in your diet. Psychobiotic bacteria in your gut also secrete and respond to neurotransmitters such as serotonin and dopamine, which are extremely important to your mental health. Trust your gut, and remember that you are what you eat!

SLEEP

Once we are able to relax, our parasympathetic nervous system can start storing energy in the brain. A study by Maiken Nedrgaard from the University of Rochester found that when we are sleeping, the glia open up and allow for toxic and waste byproducts to be removed from the brain.[76] They are discharged through the cerebrospinal fluid. The same study found this channel that removes waste byproducts from the brain is ten times more active during sleep than during waking hours.[77]

Sleep deprivation has been used as a form of torture. Anyone who has trouble sleeping might understand this a bit. Some studies have found that each hour of sleep lost per night is equal to having an alcoholic beverage. Considering that we spend about a third of our life in sleep, it is vital that we are intentional about it.

EXERCISE

Exercise helps produce better blood circulation to the brain, builds a stronger heart, a stronger body, and makes you more resilient. Spread out over each week, you need at least 150 minutes of moderate aerobic exercise or seventy-five minutes of a combination of moderate and vigorous activity. Exercise will increase the number of years in your life. You will also increase your quality of life. Exercise will help you develop more mitochondria. Your mitochondria are what help you convert carbohydrates, fat, and protein into energy. Studies have shown that after six to eight weeks, you can increase your mitochondria by up to 50 percent.[78]

Pages and pages could be written about the importance of exercise. Our body needs to be fit and strong to function as a temple more easily. Exercise helps us connect to understanding and appreciating the limits of our body. It helps us push and expand those limits. It builds confidence and vigor that strengthens our mental and spiritual vigor. It gives us life.

There are so many resources for exercise. Yoga, walking, and physical therapy are just a few. Having a partner or group to exercise with will also help you commit to it and find joy through it.

Neuroscience and the FRUIT of the SPIRIT

The Habit of Habit Formation

Forming or breaking habits can be extremely hard. There are some excellent tools that can make it easier. Below are five that I've found to be very helpful:

1) **Start Small:** Many people give up on forming habits because they get discouraged. If you want to meditate every day, try meditating for just three minutes. If you tell yourself you want to meditate for thirty minutes per day and then give up when it's too hard, you've accomplished nothing. It's much better to start small. Then you can build your way up to your goal.

2) **Isolate the Reward:** Neurologically, habits work in a loop structure containing a cue, routine, and reward. If you are watching traumatic news, it can help to take a step back and ask why. If the reward is a sense of connection, you can find that reward better with friends, family, and community than watching the news. If you can label the reward, you can change your routine to better reward what you are really looking for rather than something damaging. If you take a break to smoke a cigarette, perhaps the reward is more truly to connect with friends and have time away from stress. Isolate the reward and you can change the routine.

3) **Delay:** If your goal is to eat healthier or stop smoking, intentionally delaying your bad habit can help. If you can delay having a cigarette for five minutes or delay eating a bag of chips, then you can probably delay it ten minutes. You can build up to not doing the habit at all.

4) **Cues:** Cues are a way of helping you remember to do your habit. If you want to go to the gym in the morning, you can cue yourself by having your gym clothes all packed and ready the night before. Any small thing that can make doing the habit just a little easier might make the difference to help the habit stick.

5) **Track:** There is quite a bit of research showing that when habits are tracked, they are more successful. Taking the time to look at what you do throughout the day or week can be very

enlightening. The Daily Examen reflection in chapter 9 will help you claim and identify how the fruit of the Spirit is working in you or not working in you. Just as in Nehemiah's time when the temple walls were able to be reconstructed, so too can we reconstruct the temple of our bodies to make and be lasting change. After you have practiced new habits for months or even years, it can be very reassuring to look back and track how much progress you have made.

Mastery of the Self: Creating a Rule of Life

> A Rule of Life is an intentional pattern of spiritual disciplines that provides structure and direction for growth in holiness. ~
> C. S. Lewis Institute

Neurons that fire together wire together. When our goals become actions, they also become engrained in our neurophysiology so that our lives are a habitual expression of love, joy, and peace. At the end of each previous chapter, there was a focus question about your goal to create more of the fruit of the Spirit in your life. When a goal becomes a habit, it also becomes a part of a Rule of Life. When mastering the self, we need structure and direction. Below is an opportunity for you to look back on each of the goals that you set for yourself and track how your life has become a greater expression of the fruit of the Spirit.

In what specific ways over the last week, month, or year have I grown in God's love and overcome indifference?

_____

_____

_____

Neuroscience and the FRUIT of the SPIRIT

A tool that has helped me find or strengthen love in my life is: (example: a feelings journal, the SIBAM method, etc.)

_____

_____

_____

In what specific ways over the last week, month, or year have I grown in God's joy and away from cravings and addiction?

_____

_____

_____

A tool that has helped me find or strengthen joy in my life is: (example: playfulness, friends, finding flow through creative expression, etc.)

_____

_____

_____

In what specific ways over the last week, month, or year have I grown in God's peace instead of anxiety and worry?

_____

_____

A tool that has helped me find or strengthen peace in my life is: (example: mindfulness, Centering Prayer, awe, wonder, etc.)

_____

_____

_____

In what specific ways over the last week, month, or year have I grown in God's patience rather than despair?

_____

_____

_____

A tool from this book that has helped me find or strengthen patience in my life is: (example: specific, measurable, and relevant goals [SMART goals], etc.)

_____

_____

_____

Neuroscience and the FRUIT of the SPIRIT

In what specific ways over the last week, month, or year have I grown in God's kindness instead of hatred and strife?

_____

_____

_____

A tool from this book that has helped me find or strengthen kindness in my life is: (example: corporal works of mercy, *Forces for Good*, loving those who are different from you, loving your enemies, etc.)

_____

_____

_____

In what specific ways over the last week, month, or year have I grown in God's goodness instead of ignorance?

_____

_____

_____

Chapter 11 - Self-Control vs. Volatility

A tool from this book that has helped me find or strengthen goodness in my life is: (example: Johari window, the ABCD cognitive behavior therapy method, etc.)

_____

_____

_____

In what specific ways over the last week, month, or year have I grown in God's faithfulness rather than a life of falsehood?

_____

_____

_____

A tool that has helped me find or strengthen faithfulness in my life is: (example: The Daily Examen, deeper reflection and commitment to the Lord's Prayer, etc.)

_____

_____

_____

Neuroscience and the FRUIT of the SPIRIT

In what specific ways over the last week, month, or year have I grown in God's gentleness as opposed to hardness and prejudice?

_____

_____

_____

A tool that has helped me find or strengthen gentleness in my life is: (example: active listening skills, observing from the balcony, etc.)

_____

_____

_____

In what specific ways over the last week, month, or year have I grown in God's self-control versus volatility?

_____

_____

_____

Chapter 11 - Self-Control vs. Volatility

A tool that has helped me find or strengthen self-control in my life is: (example: exercise, nutrition, hydration, tracking habit cues and rewards, etc.)

_____

_____

_____

Looking back on my life, I can see much growth and change since I decided to follow Jesus in the way of love. There is always more room to grow and much to learn. I hope that we can look back on our lives in the future and see how much more life God has given us through following Him. May we bless God, and may God bless us!

chapter 12
Your Story Is Part of God's Story

Stories surround each of us. Our families have stories. Our neighborhoods and communities have stories. Our nation has a story. The sum of all past events falls together in a great history.

Many competing forces pull and tug on our stories, mapping them one way or the other. One group tries to write history one way while another tries to write it differently. Some people want to deny our stories. Others simply ignore our stories. People are seen as not enough or broken or a waste of space and time. The horror in our world is so overwhelming that many of us would like to hide from it. The real stories behind what is really going on in the world become hidden.

But God's story is above all this. God's story courses through every bit of it. God's story redeems what is broken. We are called to be a part of this grand adventure. God's story is a tale of righteousness and truth. God's story is a love story in the very best sense.

In the depths of darkness during the civil rights movement, Martin Luther King Jr. was feeling lost and troubled. He once got a call around midnight from someone who called him the N-word. Someone who said that he was tired of King's mess. Someone who said that he would blow out King's brains and blow up his house.

In the midst of this terror, King knelt and prayed. He heard the voice of Jesus say, "Stand up for righteousness. Stand up for truth.

Stand up for justice, and lo I will be with you even until the end of the age."[79]

That voice speaks to us. That is the call of God's story. God's story is a love story of justice, truth, and righteousness. Whatever horror, whatever mistakes, whoever you have thought you have been, it is all in the past. The story that you may have convinced yourself of, the story that someone else tried to convince you of, is not your story if it does not serve justice, truth, and love.

A new reality awaits us. Be transformed by God's goodness and let go of the horror and terror that you or anyone else is telling you. Your story is part of the great story. And it is marvelous.

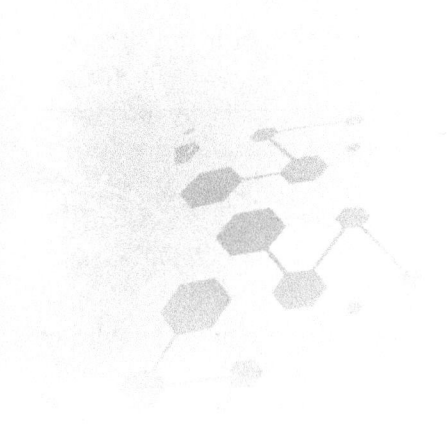

chapter 13
Group Discussion

This book is an excellent tool for a weekly adult formation class, an Advent series, Lenten series, or a book club. A small group setting can be a safe space that encourages each person to share their story, help build rapport, grow together, and feel that we are each a fellow pilgrim traversing the difficulties of life. It could be helpful to recommend reading the whole book before meeting or to work through each section together week by week. Ideally, a nine-week program is recommended where each week, the group goes deeply to examine one of the nine fruit of the Spirit. Each meeting, there is an accompanying video for the fruit of the Spirit and paired opposite on www.neurotheology.info. These include "Love vs. Indifference," "Joy vs. Addiction," and so on. Watching each video together as a group can help spark conversation.

It is helpful to consider the group's size—too large, and sharing will be difficult. If you are hosting an adult formation class, you can have several tables so that each group is not too large. The course could also be done online through Zoom.

FACILITATOR

It is recommended that the group facilitator has led a small group before or is someone who can be trusted to maintain boundaries. This will help keep the group focused and produce good fruit together. If you have multiple tables of participants, you will need a facilitator at each table. This person should help invite others to participate, especially if they have not yet shared. A facilitator will be aware of nonverbal cues, especially if it looks as if someone wants to share. They can help make space for them to do so. A small group leader keeps the group on target with time. A facilitator helps the group follow the norms that they set for themselves.[80]

GROUP NORMS

When a small group comes together, setting established expectations and boundaries can help everyone feel safe. These can be recorded, written, or even distributed after the first meeting so that everyone has easy access to expectations. The facilitator should feel empowered to help maintain the norms.

Common group norms include using "I" statements so as not to project feelings on others or try to fix them. These include things like, "In my experience, I feel . . ." or "I get anxious when . . ." When people share how bad fruit are working through them, we can listen and allow them to find the strength to overcome their bad habits. Members of the group are not encouraged to fix one another.

The group discussion focus questions are meant as active listening tools to drive deeper reflection. The group members should refrain from using their personal experiences or opinions to fix others. The power of listening and being heard is very transformative. When in small group discussions, no one should dominate the time. Encourage others to speak if they have not spoken already. Allow each member to pass if they do not feel comfortable answering. They can simply say, "Pass."

Agree to keep the discussion confidential, open, and free. Sharing someone else's personal reflection or confession outside with the general public can be very damaging. Be sure to get confirmation from group members whether sharing their reflections is okay with them.

Agree on whether cell phones are to be silenced, turned off, or available for emergencies. These are just some ways to ensure a group will have better cohesion and trust. With better cohesion and trust, the Holy Spirit has more room to work.

Neuroscience and the FRUIT of the SPIRIT

MUTUAL INVITATION

When group members are together, the facilitator can invite someone who has not gone first previously to reflect on a focus question or check in. Once the person has shared, they can then invite someone else until all have shared. This helps shift the power of a group away from just one person.

AGENDA

Meal (30 minutes)
For group discussion, it is often helpful to meet over a meal and to break bread together. It's optional though highly recommended as it builds excellent rapport.

Check-In (15 minutes)
When inviting others to share, remember to use the mutual invitation. Group participants should be allowed to pass if they would like. This provides a sense of safety. If someone passes, they can be given a time after everyone else has shared if they would like to share something of their own.

Chapter Questions (45 minutes)
At the end of each chapter, there are focus questions to help dive deep into the fruit of the Spirit. It is recommended to focus on one chapter per week, as well as the focus questions for that chapter. For group discussion, small groups should have adequate time to reflect and share about the individual questions at the end of each section. If one particular question is of greater interest or has more energy around it than others, it is not important to get to every question. It can be helpful to invite everyone to think about a particular question silently for several minutes before coming back to the group.

Check-Out (5–10 minutes)
The group members can be invited to share how they felt God was at work among them. Where did they feel the least or greatest energy? Closing with a prayer will help mark the time that was spent together as sacred. Group

members can alternate who leads prayer at the end of the meeting to ensure more voices are heard.

OTHER ITEMS TO CONSIDER

Logistical concerns such as when and where to hold meetings, how often to meet (weekly or monthly), who will bring food if there is a meal, whether to use name tags, or how to RSVP are all important items to consider.

If the group has chosen to read the entire book first, people may like to share how they are using the tools and resources when they check in at each weekly meeting. Another possibility is to have the group meet several months after the series is complete as a sort of check-in with group members so that they can share their progress.

There are many ways this book could be adapted for group discussion. May the Holy Spirit inspire you to produce fruit of love, joy, and peace that will last!

Bibliography of Recommended Reading

Beck, Judith. *Cognitive Therapy: Basics and Beyond*. New York: Guilford, 1995.

Benedict XVI [Joseph A Ratzinger]. *Jesus of Nazareth: From the Baptism in the Jordan to the Transfiguration*. San Francisco: Ignatius, 2007.

Bonhoeffer, Dietrich. *The Cost of Discipleship*. New York: Touchstone, 1959.

Bridges, Jerry. *The Fruitful Life*. Carol Stream, IL: NavPress, 2006.

Bulkeley, Kelly. *The Wondering Brain: Thinking about Religion with and Beyond Cognitive Neuroscience*. New York: Routledge, 2005.

Carter, Rita. *The Human Brain Book*. New York: DK, 2009.

Chapman, Gary. *The Five Love Languages: How to Express Heartfelt Commitment to Your Mate*. Chicago: Northland, 1992.

Cloud, Henry, & John Townsend. *Boundaries: When to Say Yes, How to Say No to Take Control of Your Life*. Grand Rapids, MI: Zondervan, 1992.

Covey, Stephen. *The 7 Habits of Highly Effective People: Powerful Lessons in Personal Change*. New York: Simon & Schuster, 2013.

de Mello, Anthony. *Sadhana: A Way to God*. New York: Image, 1978.

Foster, Richard J. *Celebration of Discipline: The Path to Spiritual Growth.* New York: Harper & Row, 1978.

Frankl, Viktor. *Man's Search for Meaning.* New York: Touchstone, 1959.

Goleman, Daniel. *Emotional intelligence: Why It Can Matter More than IQ.* New York: Bantam, 2005.

———. *Social Intelligence: The New Science of Human Relationships.* New York: Bantam, 2006.

Goleman, Daniel, & Richard J. Davidson. *Altered Traits: Science Reveals How Meditation Changes Your Mind, Brain, and Body.* New York: Avery, 2017.

Gortner, David. *Transforming Evangelism.* New York: Church Publishing, 2008.

Graham, Linda. *Bouncing Back: Rewiring Your Brain for Maximum Resilience and Well-Being.* Novato, California: New World Library, 2013.

Gutierrez, Gustavo. *A Theology of Liberation: History, Politics, and Salvation.* Maryknoll: Orbis, 1988.

Heschel, Abraham Joshua. *The Sabbath.* New York: Farrar, Straus and Giroux, 1951.

Jennings, Timothy R. *The God-Shaped Brain: How Changing Your View of God Transforms Your Life.* Downers Grove, IL: InterVarsity Press, 2013.

Kleiner, Art, Jeffrey Schwartz, and Josie Thomson. *The Wise Advocate: The Inner Voice of Strategic Leadership.* New York: Columbia University Press, 2019.

Linthicum, Dorothy, and Janice Hicks. *Redeeming Dementia: Spirituality, Theology and Science.* New York: Church Publishing, 2018.

Moore, Beth. *Living Beyond Yourself.* Nashville, TN: LifeWay Press, 1998.

Newberg, Andrew B., & Mark Robert Waldman. *How God Changes Your Brain: Breakthrough Findings from a Leading Neuroscientist.* New York: Ballantine, 2009.

O'Connor, Richard. *Rewire: Change Your Brain to Break Bad Habits, Overcome Addictions, Conquer Self-Destructive Behavior.* New York: Plume, 2014.

Oliver, Mary. *New and Selected Poems.* Boston: Beacon Press, 1992.

Rottgers, Steven R. *I am Yours!* Lindon, UT: Vervante, 2005.

Schwartz, Jeffrey M., and Rebecca Gladding. *You Are Not Your Brain: The 4-Step Solution for Changing Bad Habits, Ending Unhealthy Thinking, and Taking Control of Your Life.* New York: Avery, 2012.

Siegel, Daniel J., and Tina Payne Bryson. *The Whole-Brain Child: 12 Revolutionary Strategies to Nurture Your Child's Developing Mind.* New York: Bantam, 2011.

Thompson, Curt. *Anatomy of the Soul: Surprising Connections between Neuroscience and Spiritual Practices That Can Transform Your Life and Relationships.* Carol Stream, IL: Tyndale, 2010.

van der Kolk, Bessel. *The Body Keeps the Score: Brain, Mind, and Body in the Healing of Trauma.* New York: Penguin, 2014.

Wright, N. T. *The Lord and His prayer.* Grand Rapids, MI: Eerdmans, 1996.

———. *Paul: A Biography.* Minneapolis: Fortress Press, 2005.

Glossary

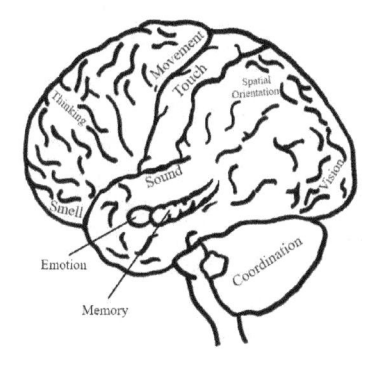

Brain diagram with labels: Movement, Touch, Spatial Orientation, Thinking, Sound, Vision, Smell, Emotion, Memory, Coordination

While there are certain parts of the brain more associated with particular tasks, we function as an integrated system. Just as each of us is an important part of the body of Christ, so too is each part of the body and brain important. (See 1 Corinthians 12:27.)

***

amygdala: An almond-shaped cluster within the limbic system of the brain. The amygdala is responsible for the detection and response to threats. When our senses are stimulated, the amygdala helps to assign emotional significance ranging from love to fear or anger. When an emotional stimulus is out of proportion with our response to it, this process is called an amygdala hijack. Just like a hammer might only see nails, if we allow ourselves to stop thinking with our prefrontal cortex and see the world as a threat, then we may opt to fight against it. Anger is often the result of fear. When not regulated, it can create the sense of a frightening authoritative God.

anterior cingulate cortex (ACC): The ACC plays a significant part in the process of emotions and helps you process God as kind and loving. It regulates spiritual anxiety, guilt, anger, and fear. It helps in your understanding of empathy and compassion. Self-discipline and acts of love will strengthen the ACC. Intense and prolonged fear or addictions will weaken it. It plays a large role in listening to the brain's circuitry toward the fear response or choosing the governance of the prefrontal cortex's inhibition of the limbic system. As such, it is a mediator between your feelings and your thoughts. A stronger ACC will help slow down the amygdala's role in the fear response.

autonomic nervous system (ANS): The two main branches of the autonomic nervous system are the parasympathetic and sympathetic nervous systems. They play very active roles in our experience of emotion. The parasympathetic nervous system (PNS) functions with our body's efforts to rest and digest. When we rest, more blood goes to our belly to digest food. We are more emotionally calm. A good metaphor is to think of it as our body's *brake* system. The sympathetic nervous system (SNS) is more involved in our body working to fight, take flight, or to freeze under stress. It helps for a quick release of energy. It is more of an *accelerator* system. Activation of the sympathetic nervous system (SNS) might increase heart rate, sweat, and muscle tone as the body readies to fight, though many of us are unaware of our own bodies responding in these ways. The work of either of the two main branches of the ANS is often unconscious. Sadness, grief, or shame might draw us into a more lethargic state such as that of the parasympathetic nervous system working in low arousal. Muscles slack, heart rate is lower, and breathing is shallower when the PNS is engaged. Emotions of rage, fear, anger, and excitement are much more associated with the sympathetic nervous system's fight and flight activation.[81] The amygdala and the body's stress response system are also involved in the SNS. By becoming more aware of our bodies, we become more aware of our emotional life and the life of the world. We also become more aware of how the fruit of the Spirit is working inside of us or how bad fruits are working inside of us.

axons and dendrites: Neurons have projections called dendrites that bring information to them from other cells and generally longer projections called axons that take information away. Research shows the more you use your brain, the better it is at maintaining and creating new axon and dendrite connections.

Neuroscience and the FRUIT of the SPIRIT

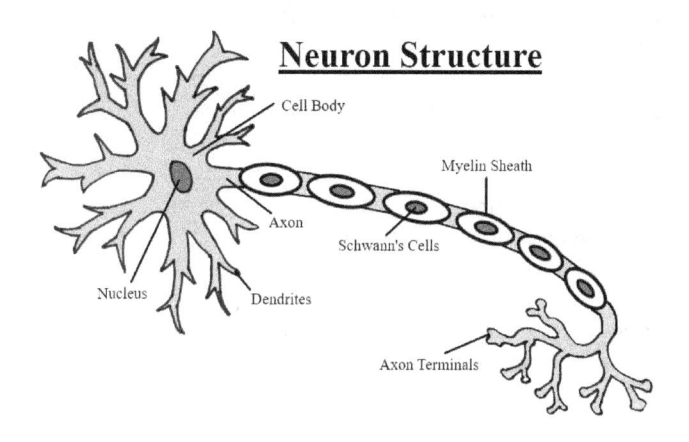

Neuron Structure

Cell Body, Myelin Sheath, Axon, Schwann's Cells, Nucleus, Dendrites, Axon Terminals

basal ganglia: The habit center of the brain, the basal ganglia are central to your automatic habitual actions and ways of thinking. Two of its major structures are the caudate and the putamen.[82] Another important component of the basal ganglia is the nucleus accumbens, which plays a critical part of our reward system.

brain waves (neural oscillations): Can be measured with electroencephalography (EEG) for frequency, amplitude, and phase. Higher frequency is associated with greater neuronal synchronization. A highly synchronized brain will have more highly synchronized brain waves.

- delta (1–4 oscillations per second): Delta waves are most present during sleep.
- theta (4–8 oscillations per second): Theta can be seen when we are drowsy.
- alpha (8–12 oscillations per second): Alpha waves are present during relaxed wakefulness, such as daydreaming.
- beta (13–30 oscillations per second): Beta waves can be seen when the brain is alert and concentrated.
- gamma (above 30 oscillations per second): Gamma waves are the highest frequency brain waves and are generally very shortly sustained. Perhaps from a sudden insight or through the realization of a taste of a favorite food, there will be spikes in gamma waves. Intense and prolonged concentration on God's love and compassion will increase the brain's ability to have sustained gamma waves.

cerebellum: Once thought to be primarily for motor function, it is now being found to be involved in attention, musical rhythm, and language processing. The act of play relates to the rate and size of growth of the cerebellum, indicating that the joy of play is integral to our survival.

cortisol: Also known as the stress hormone, cortisol helps to provide immediate glucose energy to the bloodstream. It is released to the response of threat or perceived threat. Extreme and continual exposure to cortisol is adverse to good health.

epigenetics: Genes can literally be turned on or off in utero as a baby develops. Trauma can be passed on from one generation to the next even before birth.

explicit memory: Conscious memory. The prefrontal cortex is home to your explicit memory. Either in recalling facts or experiences, your explicit memory is intentional. Implicit memory, on the other hand, is unconscious memory.

frontal lobe: Integrates the what, why, and where issues about God. It is the seat of the logic that we use about God. It will also help dictate your relationship with God. See also prefrontal cortex.

fusiform face area: Each one of us is fearfully and wonderfully made. That we are not all the same is extremely profound. There is a part of the brain, the fusiform face area, that helps us distinguish the uniqueness of others, especially by their faces. It is located on the underside of the temporal lobe. Each one of us is wonderfully made, and God has given us the gift to help recognize it.

Hebb's Law: Neurons that fire together wire together. When we practice something, our neural circuitry strengthens in helping us to remember and carry it out into the future. The more that our neural circuits fire together in healthy ways, the stronger these pathways become. Seek, and ye shall find; rewire, and the world will open up.

hemispheres: The brain is divided into two hemispheres, the left and the right. The two hemispheres are connected by a tract of approximately two hundred million fibers called the corpus callosum. The left hemisphere controls the right side of the body, and the right hemisphere controls the left side. The right hemisphere is better at holistic perception and creative processing. The left hemisphere is more attuned to logic and language processing in most people. It is a mistake to think that the left side of the brain is for logic, and the right side is for creativity. Many studies have shown

Neuroscience and the FRUIT of the SPIRIT

that both sides of the brain participate in all mental processes.[83] Author Iain McGilchrist advocates that for society to flourish, short-sighted abstraction needs to be integrated with a larger holistic perspective. Parts must be integrated with the whole just as abstract logic needs to be integrated with our incarnated reality.

hippocampus: The region of the brain associated with learning and memory. Interestingly, the hippocampus not only helps us remember the past, it also is integral to making sense of our future narrative. Those who have had their hippocampus removed not only don't remember the past but cannot project a narrative for their future. The hippocampus also processes the rise of stress hormones. It plays the role of telling the hypothalamus to stop producing the stress response. It is itself sensitive to the effects of stress. The hippocampus interacts with the amygdala to remember emotionally significant things, so it also plays an important part in our emotional responses. Chronic stress has been shown to shrink the hippocampus as well as its response in helping stop the cycle of stress.

HPA axis: The hypothalamus, pituitary, and adrenal glands make up the HPA axis, which plays a major role in the stress response. In fear or anger, the hypothalamus releases corticotropin-releasing hormone to the pituitary gland. The pituitary then sends adrenocorticotropic hormones to the adrenal glands to release cortisol, the stress hormone. Cortisol is a glucocorticoid hormone. It functions to metabolize fat, protein, and carbohydrates. The stress response allows for energy to be converted quickly. Think about what goes on in your body when you are stressed. Your blood pressure goes up, heart rate increases, and glucose is dumped into your system. In fear, we get ready to fight or take flight.

implicit memory: It is memory that is unconscious and procedural. Examples of unconscious procedural memory are tying your shoes or riding a bicycle. Once you've learned, you don't have to consciously remember each part of the process. Some neuroscientists believe that as much as 80 percent of our memory is unconscious. This might sound like a tremendous amount, but if you have ever experienced the grief of someone you love deeply dying, you will probably understand. When a person you love and who was close to you dies, there are so many daily habitual reminders of their presence that will continue to cause pain over and over unconsciously. You might even think in one moment about how sad it is that they have died and then ten minutes later habitually be reminded that it is time to start making their dinner.

insula: The insula helps us interpret our emotions. Imaging has shown that the right frontal insular cortex connects with an ability to empathize with the pain of others. Imaging also shows that it plays a role in the ability to feel one's own body, such as the heartbeat. It helps us with greater self-awareness through connecting how our emotions are processed in the body. The frontal insular is especially known for its concentration of spindle neurons. Spindle neurons are known for empathy and emotional feelings.

limbic system: It is most frequently linked to the role in emotion. It lies just under the cerebral cortex. The amygdala, hypothalamus, and hippocampus are all more commonly known parts of the limbic system.

mirror neurons: Stimulated when observing another person perform a task as if we are performing the task ourselves. Neurons fire exactly as if making the movement yourself instead of simply observing it happen. Mirror neuron systems in the brain allow us to understand the actions and intentions of others. The better our minds understand how others act and intend, the better we can learn from them. Unless we develop our own capacity to understand and appreciate the actions of others, we will not have the empathy necessary to engage the world in love. Mirror neurons come into play when we recognize facial expressions. You might be able to recall a time in your life where you saw someone get hurt and noticed that you cringed your shoulders as if you somehow felt the pain as well. Imagine for a moment, someone smiling at you. Do you feel joy? Perhaps it will make you smile as well. This is an example of mirror neurons at work. In fact, basic emotional states expressed cross-culturally are extremely similar. Anger, boredom, worry, joy, and fear can be identified in people in vastly different cultures simply by looking at their faces.

neuroplasticity: Neuroscience is finding that our minds are capable of great change. For a long time, it was believed that older people could not rewire their brains through new learning. It was believed that habits were more ingrained. Neuroscience is now finding that the brain has the capacity to rewire itself even into our advanced years.

neurotheology: The scientific study of how spiritual beliefs, religious practices, and experiences have connection to and influence our neurological make up.

neurotransmitters: Nerve cells communicate with one another through chemicals called neurotransmitters. The various neurotransmitters have very distinct functions.

- Acetylcholine is involved in higher processing and mental function. Abstract thought and mental deductions of theological reflection are thought to be influenced by acetylcholine.

Neuroscience and the FRUIT of the SPIRIT

- Serotonin plays a large part in mood. Low serotonin levels have been linked to depression, where moderately increased levels lead to a more positive outlook.
- Beta-endorphins depress fear, reduce pain, and produce sensations of euphoria. Play generates endorphins, which make you feel good. Exercise also helps produce endorphins.
- Dopamine is a neurotransmitter associated with reward. In the frontal cortex, dopamine will help us work toward our desired goals. It will also help with decision-making. Dopamine will help us feel rewarded in our pursuit of meaning and purpose. Healthy levels of dopamine will help us with motivation and the pursuit of desires. It is vitally important to us. Unhealthy levels of dopamine can lead to addiction characterized by abuse, dependency, and pathological craving.
- Gamma-aminobutyric acid (GABA) plays a role in "turning off" certain parts of the brain. In meditation and prayer, GABA likely plays a role in turning down excitatory states. Stretching and yoga have also been found to increase GABA, which may lower anxiety and depression.
- Oxytocin is a neurotransmitter that plays a large role in social bonding. Oxytocin helps play in the role of our feeling safe and secure. The release of oxytocin from the hypothalamus helps drop the level of cortisol stress hormones. This also helps blood pressure drop. A soothing and warm touch helps the process unfold; however, it is not necessary to have touch. The connection of your mind and heart to remembering that you are loved and connected also has a similar effect.

neurotrophic factors (NTFs): A class of biomolecules that help in the growth and sustenance of our neurons. They are responsible for axon growth and regeneration. They are a large part of what makes neuroplasticity possible.

nucleus accumbens: The heart of the reward system of the brain and works in conjunction with the neurochemical dopamine. Dopamine is released from the nucleus accumbens. Unhealthy levels of dopamine can lead to addiction characterized by abuse, dependency, and pathological craving. An addict who continually abuses through overstimulating will numb the pleasure response and make the reward circuit turn on itself. When overstimulated, the nucleus accumbens, through a binding protein known as CREB (cAMP response element-binding protein), activates the release of dynorphin. Dynorphin inhibits overstimulation of the nucleus accumbens. What happens with addiction is that over time the feeling of pleasure decreases just as craving increases, because the brain is naturally trying to limit overstimulation.

parietal lobe: One of the four lobes of the cerebral cortex. Helps establish our understanding of self in relation to space, time, and objects. A decrease in activity in the parietal lobe leads to an increased sense of selflessness. There is more of an awareness of "we" rather than simply "I."

parietal-frontal circuit: Helps establish God's presence and allows for perception of God in space. It draws together the connection between the distinction of God and self. A decrease in activity in the parietal lobe leads to an increased sense of selflessness. Separation from God decreases. The parietal-frontal circuit, in particular, helps establish a relationship between our conceptions of self and God. It helps establish the feeling of God's presence in time and space, as well as our connection to this reality.

pituitary gland: is part of an axis that releases hormones from the adrenal glands during the stress response. Specifically, hormones from the pituitary gland drive the adrenal glands situated on top of the kidneys.

precuneus: Is believed to play a role in consciousness and self-awareness.[84] It plays a role with memory in creating context with past experience.

prefrontal cortex: Plays a role in restraining the limbic system. The prefrontal cortex is also the seat of our executive decision-making. It helps predict how we integrate our understanding of God. It creates the logic used to develop our conceptions of God. It works at answering the most challenging questions about the nature of God: What is God? Why does God do or not do something?

- Dorsolateral prefrontal cortex (DLPFC) is associated with reasoning, planning, and executive function. It has a prolonged maturation into adulthood.
- Orbitofrontal cortex (OFC) is associated with inhibiting inappropriate social behaviors. It works in conjunction with the anterior cingulate cortex (ACC) especially regarding coordination of emotional reaction.
- Ventromedial prefrontal cortex (VMPFC) is involved in moral and ethical decision-making as well as making meaning of life. It has been shown to have decreased activity with depression and increased activity with mania.

Neuroscience and the FRUIT of the SPIRIT

somatic nervous system: Unlike the autonomic nervous system, which is involuntary, the somatic nervous system is voluntary. It is the seat of conscious control of muscles and nerves. Intentionally reading this glossary right now is part of your conscious somatic nervous system that signals nerves and small muscles to cause your eyes to sweep across the text.

spindle neurons: also known as von Economo neurons (VENs) from Constantin von Economo's 1926 discovery. They are fast and large for a fast relay of social interconnectedness. They have only been found in a handful of species outside of humans including whales, dolphins, elephants, and monkeys. They are thought to play a role in intuition and social interactions. They are more developed in species with complex social systems. They have been found in the anterior cingulate cortex (ACC), the fronto-insular cortex (FI), and the dorsolateral prefrontal cortex (DLPFC).

somatosensory cortex: This area of the parietal lobe provides us a connection with the sensory feeling of the different areas of our bodies such as the face, lips, hands, legs, and feet. It receives sensory information through the thalamus. The somatosensory cortex has more content and skill at feeling highly sensitive areas such as the hands and face as opposed to the legs or back. Take a moment to purse your lips and you will notice that you have much more ability to detect each area around your mouth than you would if you concentrated on feeling the sensations in your elbow.

striatum: Is central to our automatic thoughts and actions. It is the largest structure of the basal ganglia and includes the nucleus accumbens, putamen, and caudate. It inhibits the activity of the amygdala. It allows you to feel safe in the presence of God.[85]

thalamus: Plays a role in our sense of reality, of what is real. It connects emotional meaning to our conception of God. It is largely responsible for helping us feel that God is real in an objective sense. Of enormous consequence, the more you strengthen an idea over and over, the brain responds as if the idea is real within the world. The thalamus doesn't make a distinction between inner and outer realities. Belief can become neurologically real, for better or worse.

vagus nerve: Also called the tenth cranial nerve, it regulates the autonomic nervous system in three primary states: 1) ventral vagal complex (VVC), which cues social engagement; 2) the sympathetic nervous system (SNS), which responds as fight or flight; and 3) dorsal vagal complex (DVC), which signals the body to freeze, withdrawing in collapse, usually when confronting extreme danger. The vagus nerve has two branches, the ventral and dorsal branch.

When we are able to feel safe and calm, the autonomic system operates through the integration of the ventral branch of the vagus nerve. We have relaxed muscles, we're able to be social and engage others, blood flows to the skin, and we are capable of pleasurable emotions. We have access to our prefrontal cortex when we feel safe and calm. Especially in the event of trauma, the dorsal branch gets activated. When an event either is or seems so threatening that we become overwhelmed, it can cause the body to freeze and go into collapse. The body becomes flaccid, heart rate slows, breathing is shallow, and we become disassociated with our executive function. It is a state that can mimic death. These two branches of the vagus nerve create what is known as the polyvagal theory, developed by Steven Porges. The ventral branch (at the front of the body) is activated when we are calm. The dorsal branch (at the back of the body) is activated when we are so overwhelmed that the body freezes and collapses.

ventral tegmentum area (VTA): Dopamine is released from the VTA as well as the nucleus accumbens. It is part of the reward circuit of the brain. The VTA fires when an unexpected or surprising reward is discovered. The VTA helps in remembering new rewards that are different from our previous expectations.

Index

acetylcholine, 186
addiction, 30, 61-68
adverse childhood experiences, 40, 88, 101
amygdala, 32-34, 43, 76, 77, 85, 100, 101, 137, 181
anterior cingulate, 32-34, 43, 85, 86, 114, 159, 182
anxiety, 32, 35, 72, 76-78, 81, 82, 85, 159, 182
attachment theory, 39
autonomic nervous system, 43, 182
awe, 45, 75, 76
axons, 15, 182
basal ganglia, 158, 183
belief, 32, 89, 116, 117, 123, 127-132
brain waves, 73, 183
Butterfly Effect, 21, 22, 64, 65, 103, 112
Centering Prayer, 74
cerebellum, 34, 59, 184
cognitive behavioral therapy, 116-119
cognitive distortions, 117-119
cortisol, 36, 76, 88, 99, 100, 184

Daily Examen, 139-142
default mode network (DMN), 71, 76
dendrites, 15, 182
desperation, 87-89, 93
dopamine, 61-63, 158, 161, 187
dorsolateral prefrontal cortex, 33, 34, 58, 85, 125, 188
endorphins, 58, 99, 187
epigenetics, 88, 184
explicit memory, 184
falsehood, 110, 113, 115, 137, 138, 144-146
flow state, 56-58
forgiveness, 101, 102, 139, 140, 148
frontal lobe, 33, 34, 38, 59, 184
fusiform face area, 20, 184
gamma-aminobutryic acid (GABA), 159, 187
grace, 23-25, 27, 38, 54, 86, 114, 127, 128, 140
habits, 14, 15, 50, 116, 119, 124, 157-164, 183
hatred, 88, 89, 100- 102, 106-108
heaven, 114, 124, 133
Hebb's Law, 15, 85, 158, 184

hell, 133
hemispheres, 184
hippocampus, 34, 77, 113, 148, 159, 185
HPA Axis, 76, 185
ignorance, 110-119, 121
implicit memory, 72, 158, 185
insula, 34, 35, 43, 73, 74, 185
Johari Window, 110
limbic system, 186
medial prefrontal cortex, 34, 42, 114, 149
mindfulness, 71
mirror neurons, 55, 99, 100, 103, 186
neuroplasticity, 14, 186
neurotheology, 186
neurotransmitters, 161, 186
nucleus accumbens, 61, 62, 137, 158, 183, 187
orbitofrontal cortex, 33, 34, 85, 114, 125, 188
oxytocin, 36, 99, 187
parasympathetic nervous system (PNS), 43, 44, 162, 182
parietal lobe, 34, 37-38, 74, 188
pituitary gland, 76, 188
play, 59, 60, 184
preaching, 135, 136
precuneus, 188
prefrontal cortex, 32-34, 36, 62, 85, 88, 90, 101, 113, 114, 125, 129, 188
prejudice, 112, 114, 149, 150, 154, 155
priming, 72
serotonin, 58, 99, 161, 187
SIBAM, 45-48
SMART Goals, 90, 91
somatic nervous system, 44, 189
somatosensory cortex, 34, 189
spindle neurons, 186, 189
stress, 36, 41, 43, 58, 63, 76, 77, 88, 99, 113, 159, 182, 184, 185
striatum, 149, 189
sympathetic nervous system (SNS), 43, 44, 182, 189
thalamus, 34, 55, 56, 72, 115, 137, 189
unconscious bias, 110-112, 149
vagus nerve, 85, 87, 189
ventral tegmentum area, 61, 190
ventromedial prefrontal cortex, 33, 34, 113, 125, 188
volatility, 159, 160
von Economo neurons, 32, 189
εις, 126-132

Notes

1. You Will Know Them by Their Fruits

[1] Judith Beck, *Cognitive Therapy: Basics and Beyond* (New York: Guildford, 1995), 17.
[2] Andrew B. Newberg and Mark Robert Waldman, *How God Changes Your Brain: Breakthrough Findings from a Leading Neuroscientist* (New York: Ballantine Books, 2009), 104.

2. Your Body Is a Temple of the Holy Spirit

[3] Patrick Morley, *The Man in the Mirror: Solving the 24 Problems Men Face* (Grand Rapids, MI: Zondervan, 1997), 174.
[4] "Economy," Online Etymology Dictionary, accessed December 5, 2018, https://www.etymonline.com/word/economy.
[5] "How Many Earths Fit into the Sun?" Cornell University Astrology Department, accessed January 2, 2019, http://curious.astro.cornell.edu/about-us/36-our-solar-system/the-earth/general-questions/2-how-many-earths-fit-into-the-sun.
[6] "Hubble Reveals Observable Universe Contains 10 Times More Galaxies than Previously Thought," NASA, accessed January 2, 2019, https://www.nasa.gov/feature/goddard/2016/hubble-reveals-observable-universe-contains-10-times-more-galaxies-than-previously-thought.
[7] "How Many Stars in the Milky Way?" NASA, accessed January 2, 2019, https://asd.gsfc.nasa.gov/blueshift/index.php/2015/07/22/how-many-stars-in-the-milky-way/.
[8] Steven Rottgers, *I am Yours!* (Vervante: Springville, Utah, 2005), 21.

3. Love vs. Indifference

[9] "ἀγάπη," StudyLight, accessed April 26, 2015, http://www.studylight.org/lexicons/greek/gwview.cgi?n=26.

[10] "Eros," Online Etymology Dictionary, accessed December 5, 2018, http://www.etymonline.com/index.php?allowed_in_frame=0&search=eros&searchmode=none.

[11] "Agape," Merriam-Webster, accessed April 25, 2015, http://www.merriam-webster.com/dictionary/agape.

[12] Timothy Jennings, *The God Shaped Brain: How Changing Your View of God Transforms Your Life* (Westmont, Illinois: IVP Books, 2014), 38.

[13] Newberg and Waldman, *How God Changes Your Brain: Breakthrough Findings from a Leading Neuroscientist* (New York: Ballantine Books, 2009), 43.

[14] Mark Waldman and Chris Manning, *NeuroWisdom: The New Brain Science of Money, Happiness, and Success* (New York: Diversion Books, 2017), 69.

[15] Rita Carter, *The Human Brain Book* (New York: DK, 2019), 138.

[16] "Valentine's Day: 'Falling in Love' by Jesuit Father Pedro Arrupe," Society of Jesus, accessed August 27, 2019, https://jesuits.org/news-detail?TN=NEWS-20140210025007.

[17] Newberg and Waldman, *How God Changes Your Brain: Breakthrough Findings from a Leading Neuroscientist* (New York: Ballantine Books, 2009), 43.

[18] "אָהַב," StudyLight, accessed April 19, 2015, http://www.studylight.org/desk/interlinear.cgi?ref=02019018.

[19] Curt Thompson, *Anatomy of the Soul* (Carol Stream, IL: Tyndale, 2010), 115.

[20] Dorothy Linthicum and Janice Hicks, *Redeeming Dementia: Spirituality, Theology, and Science* (New York: Church Publishing, 2018), 43.

[21] "Global Hunger Continues to Rise, New UN Report Says," World Health Organization, accessed September 5, 2019, https://www.who.int/news-room/detail/11-09-2018-global-hunger-continues-to-rise---new-un-report-says.

[22] "*The Brain with David Eagleman*, Episode 5, 'Why Do I Need You?'" PBS, accessed October 1, 2019, https://www.pbs.org/video/brain-david-eagleman-why-do-i-need-you-episode-5/.

[23] Babette Rothschild, *The Body Remembers: Volume 2* (New York: Norton, 2017), 38.

[24] Peter Levine, *In an Unspoken Voice: How the Body Releases Trauma and Restores Goodness* (Berkeley, CA: North Atlantic, 2010), 139.

4. Joy vs. Addiction

[25] Vicktor Frankl, *Man's Search for Meaning* (New York: Touchstone, 1984), 84.
[26] "The Science of Peak Performance," Time, accessed December 5, 2018, http://time.com/56809/the-science-of-peak-human-performance/.
[27] Stuart Brown and Christopher Vaughan, *Play: How It Shapes the Brain, Opens the Imagination, and Invigorates the Soul* (New York: Avery, 2009), 34.
[28] Thad Polk, "3. How Addiction Hijacks the Brain," filmed 2015 by The Great Courses Plus, video, https://www.thegreatcoursesplus.com/the-addictive-brain.
[29] Mihaly Csikszentmihalyi, *Finding Flow: The Psychology of Engagement with Everyday Life* (New York: HarperCollins, 1997), 101.

5. Peace vs. Anxiety

[30] "Matthew 11:28," Studylight, accessed November 8, 2019, https://www.studylight.org/desk/interlinear.cgi?ref=39011028.
[31] "The Authority of Truth," My Utmost for His Highest, accessed November 11, 2019, https://utmost.org/the-authority-of-truth/.
[32] Richard O'Conner, *Rewire: Change Your Brain to Break Bad Habits, Overcome Addictions, Conquer Self-Destructive Behavior* (New York: Plume, 2014), 29.
[33] "EEG Activity in Carmelite Nuns during a Mystical Experience," National Center for Biotechnology Information, accessed August 21, 2019, https://www.ncbi.nlm.nih.gov/pubmed/18721862.
[34] Daniel Goleman and Richard Davidson, *Altered Traits: Science Reveals How Meditation Changes Your Mind, Brain, and Body* (New York: Avery, 2018), 233.
[35] Richard Davidson and Sharon Begley, *The Emotional Life of Your Brain: How Its Unique Patterns Affect the Way You Think, Feel, and Live—and How You Can Change Them* (New York: Hudson Street Press, 2010), 80.
[36] "Centering Prayer," Contemplative Outreach, accessed January 2, 2019, https://www.contemplativeoutreach.org/centering-prayer-method/
[37] "The Way of Love," The Episcopal Church, accessed August 30, 2019, https://www.episcopalchurch.org/way-of-love.

[38] "Awe and Its Benefits," Psychology Today, accessed December 5, 2018, https://www.psychologytoday.com/us/blog/understanding-awe/201704/the-emerging-science-awe-and-its-benefits.
[39] Kelly Bulkeley, *The Wondering Brain: Thinking about Religion with and Beyond Cognitive Neuroscience* (New York: Routledge, 2005), 3.
[40] Richard O'Conner, *Rewire: Change Your Brain to Break Bad Habits, Overcome Addictions, Conquer Self-Destructive Behavior* (New York: Plume, 2014), 27.

6. Patience vs. Desperation

[41] Richard Davidson and Sharon Begley, *The Emotional Life of Your Brain: How Its Unique Patterns Affect the Way You Think, Feel, and Live—and How You Can Change Them* (New York: Hudson Street Press, 2010), 72.
[42] "Desperation," Online Etymology Dictionary, accessed February 20, 2020, https://www.etymonline.com/search?q=desperation.
[43] Tula Karras, "Your Emotions: The Science of How You Feel." Special Issue, *National Geographic* (2020): 65.
[44] "How Common is PTSD in Adults?" National Center for PTSD, accessed January 2, 2019, https://www.ptsd.va.gov/understand/common/common_adults.asp.
[45] Jerry Bridges, *The Fruitful Life* (Carol Stream, IL: NavPress, 2006), 85.
[46] David Gortner, *Transforming Evangelism* (New York: Church Publishing, 2008), 136.
[47] "Regrets of the Dying," Bronnie Ware, accessed September 13, 2019, https://bronnieware.com/blog/regrets-of-the-dying/.

7. Kindness vs. Hatred

[48] "Neural Correlates of Hate," National Center for Biotechnology Information, accessed August 13, 2019, https://www.ncbi.nlm.nih.gov/pmc/articles/PMC2569212/.
[49] Lisa Sinclair, *Restoring the Paths: Sexuality for Christian Leaders* (Milwaukee, WI: T.A.L.K. Publishing, 2020), 103.
[50] Leslie Crutchfield and Heather McLeod Grant, *Forces for Good: The Six Practices of High-Impact Nonprofits* (San Francisco: Jossey-Bass, 2012), 37.

8. Goodness vs. Ignorance

[51] "Food Waste FAQs," U.S. Department of Agriculture, accessed October 1, 2019, https://www.usda.gov/foodwaste/faqs.
[52] "Debt to the Penny," accessed July 30, 2020, https://treasurydirect.gov/govt/reports/pd/pd_debttothepenny.htm.
[53] "How Gratitude Changes You and Your Brain," Greater Good Science Center at UC Berkeley, accessed August 13, 2020, https://greatergood.berkeley.edu/article/item/how_gratitude_changes_you_and_your_brain.
[54] J. S. Beck, *Cognitive Therapy: Basics and Beyond* (New York: Guilford Press, 2011), 119.

9. Faith vs. Falsehood

[55] Timothy Jennings, *The God Shaped Brain: How Changing Your View of God Transforms Your Life* (Westmont, Illinois: IVP Books, 2014), 38.
[56] "Belief, (n.)," StudyLight, accessed December 18, 2018, https://www.etymonline.com/word/belief?ref=etymonline_crossreference.
[57] "Strong's #1519 - εἰς," StudyLight, accessed modified January 31, 2019, https://www.studylight.org/lexicons/greek/1519.html.
[58] Lawrence Richards, *Expository Dictionary of Bible Words* (Grand Rapids, MI: Zondervan, 1991), 117.
[59] N. T. Wright, *Paul: A Biography* (Minneapolis: Fortress Press, 2009), 114.
[60] "Millennials' Views of News Media, Religious Organizations Grow More Negative," Pew Research Center, accessed July 14, 2020, https://www.pewresearch.org/fact-tank/2016/01/04/millennials-views-of-news-media-religious-organizations-grow-more-negative/.
[61] "In U.S., Decline of Christianity Continues at Rapid Pace," Pew Research Center, accessed November 11, 2019, https://www.pewforum.org/2019/10/17/in-u-s-decline-of-christianity-continues-at-rapid-pace/.
[62] "Hermann Ebbinghaus," Britannica, accessed July 28, 2020, https://www.britannica.com/biography/Hermann-Ebbinghaus.
[63] Richard Cox, *Rewiring Your Preaching: How the Brain Processes Sermons* (Downers Grove, IL: IVP Books, 2012), 96.
[64] Newberg and Waldman, *How God Changes Your Brain: Breakthrough Findings from a Leading Neuroscientist* (New York: Ballantine, 2009), 55.

[65] Yudhijit Bhattacharjee, "Why We Lie: The Science Behind Our Complicated Relationship with the Truth," *National Geographic* (June 2017): 47.

10. Gentleness vs. Prejudice

[66] "The Neuroscience of Prejudice and Stereotyping," ResearchGate, accessed July 10, 2018, https://www.researchgate.net/publication/265345113_The_Neuroscience_of_Prejudice_and_Stereotyping
[67] David Gortner, *Transforming Evangelism* (New York: Church Publishing, 2008), 11.
[68] Robert A. Kidd, "Foundational Listening and Responding Skills," in *Professional Spiritual & Pastoral Care: A Practical Clergy and Chaplain's Handbook*, ed. Stephen Roberts (Vermont: Skylight Paths, 2012), 92–105.

11. Self-Control vs. Volatility

[69] Linda Graham, *Bouncing Back: Rewiring Your Brain for Maximum Resilience and Well-Being* (Novato, CA: New World Library, 2013), 36.
[70] "How Habits Work," Charles Duhigg, accessed August 7, 2019, https://charlesduhigg.com/how-habits-work/.
[71] "Prediabetes: Your Chance to Prevent Type 2 Diabetes," Centers for Disease Control and Prevention, accessed August 21, 2019, https://www.cdc.gov/diabetes/basics/prediabetes.html.
[72] "Report Sets Dietary Intake Levels for Water, Salt, and Potassium to Maintain Health and Reduce Chronic Disease Risk," The National Academies of Sciences, Engineering and Medicine, accessed January 2, 2019, http://www8.nationalacademies.org/onpinews/newsitem.aspx?RecordID=10925.
[73] Mary Oliver, *New and Selected Poems* (Boston: Beacon, 1992), 38.
[74] "Your Hunger Hormones," WebMD, accessed December 5, 2018, https://www.webmd.com/diet/features/your-hunger-hormones#1.
[75] Scott Anderson, John Cryan, and Ted Dinan, *The Psychobiotic Revolution: Mood, Food, and the New Science of the Gut-Brain Connection* (Washington, DC: National Geographic, 2017), 54.
[76] "Brain May Flush Out Toxins during Sleep," National Institutes of Health, accessed December 7, 2018, https://www.nih.gov/news-events/news-releases/brain-may-flush-out-toxins-during-sleep.

[77] Norman Doidge, *The Brain's Way of Healing: Remarkable Discoveries and Recoveries from the Frontiers of Neuroplasticity* (New York: Penguin, 2015), 112.

[78] "What Happens to Your Body When You Start Exercising Regularly," accessed June 10, 2020, https://www.youtube.com/watch?v=rBUjOY12gJA.

12. Your Story is Part of God's Story

[79] "Martin Luther King Jr., 'Why Jesus Called a Man a Fool' August 27, 1967," accessed July 17, 2020, https://www.youtube.com/watch?v=xo-6BNtq5RY.

13. Group Discussion

[80] "The Way of Love: Small Group Facilitation Guide and Curriculum," The Episcopal Church, accessed September 23, 2019, https://www.episcopalchurch.org/files/documents/way_of_love_small_group_curriculum.pdf.

Glossary

[81] Babette Rothschild, *The Body Remembers: Volume 2* (New York: Norton, 2017), 38.

[82] Jeffrey Schwartz and Rebecca Gladding, *You are Not Your Brain: The 4-Step Solution for Changing Bad Habits, Ending Unhealthy Thinking, and Taking Control of Your Life* (New York: Avery, 2011), 76–77.

[83] Andrew Newberg, *Neurotheology: How Science Can Enlighten Us About Spirituality*, (New York: Columbia University Press, 2018), 56.

[84] Newberg and Waldman, *How God Changes Your Brain: Breakthrough Findings from a Leading Neuroscientist* (New York: Ballantine, 2009), 156.

[85] Ibid., 43.

For more information and resources to help you connect with how the God of love is at work within us, visit:

www.neurotheology.info

CPSIA information can be obtained
at www.ICGtesting.com
Printed in the USA
LVHW081526141220
674127LV00035B/1310